JAGUAR XJS

HIGH PERFORMANCE
·S·E·R·I·E·S·

JAGUAR XJS

RIVERS FLETCHER

CADOGAN BOOKS
LONDON

First published 1983
© Rivers Fletcher
ISBN 0 946313 45 8

Published by Cadogan Books Limited,
15 Pont Street, London SW1.

Design and Phototypesetting by Logos Design & Advertising,
Datchet, Berkshire
Printed in Great Britain by Biddles of Guildford

Dedication

To F.R.W. England. Though the XJS is not primarily a racing car, it is born of Jaguar racing and Le Mans. 'Lofty England' is all that, and all that is 'lofty England'

CONTENTS

John Egan, Chairman.

FOREWORD
– by John Egan –

When Rivers Fletcher invited me to write the foreword for this book I was delighted to accept as the XJS has a special place in my affections and is the car I drive myself whenever possible.

The market fortunes of the XJS over the past 3 years are also a perfect paradigm of what has happened in Jaguar Cars Ltd during the same period. In 1980 when I joined the company it was clear that XJS had been somewhat neglected since its launch five years previously, indeed some of the advice we received at the time questioned whether there was any future for the model. All of us at Jaguar were convinced that there was however and set about planning the launch of the new H.E. version.

The XJS H.E. was announced in July 1981 and the reception it got justified our faith. Not only did the worlds first production application of Michael May's "fireball" combustion chamber principle transform the car's fuel enconomy but also the detail changes we made to the exterior and interior specification improved its comfort and aesthetic appeal.

The XJS H.E. also incorporated the first fruits of all the hard work that everyone at Jaguar had put into improving quality and realiability over the previous year and along with the rest of the Jaguar range continues to benefit from this effort.

Market response to the H.E. was immediate and has grown steadily ever since. Sales which had fallen to 1758 in 1980 have increased to around 4500 this year and provide an excellent platform for us to launch our new 3.6 litre AJ6 engined models. I am sure that along with the H.E. which continues as the magnificent flagship of the range the XJS has a successful and secure future ahead of it.

I hope XJS enthusiasts everywhere find Rivers' personal account of the car as interesting as I did.

ACKNOWLEDGEMENTS

My first acknowledgement must be to the Jaguar Company, for the tremendous help given to me by everyone. That the Chairman, Mr John Egan, has written the foreword, is a great honour. Just as Sir Williams Lyons was 'the man' for the first 50 years of the Company – John Egan is 'the man' today. When talking to him he always plays down his part and talks about the team but of course in such a team the captain is absolutely vital.

So many people in different departments at Jaguars have given unstinting assistance in this book that I could not name them all. But David Boole, Director, Communications and Public Affairs; Arnold Bolton, Manager of Public Relations and Kim Badland the Press Officer have all been to a great deal of trouble to help me. Then there is Jim Randle, the Engineering Director and George Mason from the experimental department and the heads of all the factory departments as Browns Lane, Radford and Castle Bromwich. I could go on, but just one person at Jaguar has done so much for this book that it is really his book rather than mine – Jim Callaghan, the photographer who has worked with me throughout and taken all the photographs that show how an XJS is made. My grateful thanks to him for his patience and fine work.

Outside the Jaguar Company I have been helped by many friends, such as Philip Turner and members of the Jaguar Drivers Club, but one well known Jaguar personality, Andrew Whyte, who used to be their P.R.O. and is their great historian, has given me invaluable help and also loaned me wonderful and unique photographs. All this from another author writing about the same marque!

As with my previous books I have had every help from my private secretary Stella Tompkins, and with this book from Anne Hurst as well.

Sir William Lyons (right) founder of Jaguar with chairman John Egan on the company's 60th anniversary. Flanking them are a 1937 SS Jaguar and a current Jaguar XJ6.

Chapter One

SWALLOW DAYS
– The Early Years –

The XJS, the best and fastest big cat, is in fact the 'boss cat'. If there is an acknowledged leader of the world's supercars – then Jaguar's flag-ship the XJS H.E. is that car.

Perhaps we should try to define a 'supercar'. I think '*Autocar*' says it well, 'Supercar, soo'par-Kar, n (coll) special kind of high performance automobile, very powerful engine usually behind driver, exotic appearance, often Italian.' The XJS certainly fits, though the engine is in fact in front of the driver and of course Jaguar is very British, and proud of it.

In this book we will not try to compare its rivals, or even list them. The leading technical journals do this very well, and on nearly every count the Jaguar XJS H.E. comes out on top. I do not rate the large four-door luxury saloons as 'supercars', though some have the requisite speed, and there are a few cars with the right configuration and performance but are really sports/racing cars without luxury refinements. There are only six to ten real 'supercars,', perhaps only three from our country and the rest from the Continent.

Before we consider the car let us see how it has happened, how the Jaguar company has grown from humble beginnings to the eminent position it holds today, and how it has come to make such a car.

The first 60 years of the Jaguar story is really the success story of the life's work of one man – William, now Sir William, Lyons. Lord Montagu has chronicled this up to 1961 to the start of the E type, and there have been many more books on the various models and the racing. The E type has been well covered, by Paul Skilleter in great detail and by Denis Jenkinson in his intimate and amusing style.

Andrew Whyte, who served his apprenticeship at Jaguars and was its Public Relations Officer until Jaguar became part of British Leyland, has written the definitive biography of Jaguar right up to the present, so the marque is very well documented. I will only precis the development and add my own impressions of those times, for I was always close to the action. Never employed by Swallow Sidecars or Jaguar, but for more than fifty years seeing the company from many different angles, from the opposition as well as testing, demonstrating and selling S.S. cars, then after the war with a major supplier to Jaguars, driving all the models, owning and racing many, and filming and writing about them.

Jaguar antecedents go back to Swallow Sidecars in 1920, Swallow Sports car bodies in 1927, and the S.S. car in 1931. The Jaguar name first appeared as a type name in the S.S. Jaguar in 1936, and it was not until the end of the Second World War in 1945 that the S.S. company changed its name to Jaguar Cars Limited and the make of the car was established as Jaguar. William Lyons was the man who started it all and was the presiding genius who ran the companies until his retirement in 1972.

John Boulton, best known as a speedway writer of the 1920s, with his favourite touring combination, a Brough Superior with Swallow sidecar.

I first saw pictures of the Swallow sidecar in copies of *The Motor Cycle* and *Motor Cycling* when I was a prep schoolboy in the early 1920s. I soon saw them on the road usually with the most powerful motor cycles. An old friend, John Boulton, whom I often see these days as he is a leading official in the Bugatti Owners Club, was a well known Speedway rider racing at Belleview, White City and all the other tracks. His favourite road machine was a V twin Brough Superior with a Swallow sidecar, the most attractive combination on the road.

In 1928 before I left School, I got to know a boy a little older than myself whose father had given him a new Austin Seven Swallow for his birthday. He lived only a few miles away and though he never let me take the wheel (anyway I was under age for a driving licence) he took me for some fine runs in the holidays. That Austin Swallow was cream and red, and very sporty. The bulbous radiator cowl was polished aluminium and there was a detachable hard top which had cost an extra £10. Aged sixteen I had been mad keen on cars for several years, and in my youthful conceit I considered myself quite knowledgeable. Though I thought the Swallow was very striking I did consider that it was rather flashy. I preferred the traditional flat radiator of the other Austin Sports models to the rounded front of the Swallow and thought that its long streamlined bulbous tail less attractive than the traditional sketchy bodies on the other sports Austin Sevens.

I believed, quite incorrectly, that no streamlining was of any use at less than sixty miles an hour which was probably beyond the speed of the Austin Swallow. No wind tunnels in those days of course, and it was thought that the optimum shape of a car for racing was of tear drop configuration. The racing cars at Brooklands which sought to take advantage of the new fangled streamlining used this shape and had very long tapered tails. Amongst the Austin Sevens Boyde-Carpenter used a tear drop shape with rounded nose and long tapering tail in his car, but misguided enthusiasts like me rather scorned the relatively slow sports cars that presumed to be streamlined.

William Lyon's Swallow bodies did not pretend to be competition models, they did not ape the racers so were more honest than many of their rivals. Obviously William Lyons happened to be right with the streamlining too, the smooth shape of the Swallow body gave it an advantage both in speed and economy, but we did not realise it. In 1930 I drove several Swallow bodied Wolseley Hornets, both the two and four seater models were outstandingly beautiful, but once again I preferred the more traditional bodies like the Eustace

Charles Needham driving his 1934 S.S. I tourer at Shelsley Walsh.

Charles Needham at speed over an Alpine pass.

Watkins Daytona model and similar models by Abbey and Jarvis.

When the first S.S. cars appeared at the 1931 Motor Show at Olympia they were the sensation of the Show. William Lyons had produced a strikingly low and long sports coupé, on a new chassis with a simple side valve six cylinder Standard engine. The price of the 16 hp S.S. coupé was only £310, but it looked like a £1,000 touch.

At that time I was the junior salesman of Bentley Motors Limited, and our nearest equivalent model, the Speed Six with sports coupé coachwork, was about £3,000 – for which one could buy nine or ten S.S. coupés! Needless to say the S.S. was not madly fast and at a fraction of the price of a Bentley it was a fantastic bargain. S.S. cars sold like hot cakes, and this was the time of the recession when many well established motor manufacturers went to the wall, including my employees!

The first S.S. models had fixed cycle type wings and heavy side valances. I thought the appearance was absolutely right and was in fact rather disappointed that the later models used long sweeping wings merging into the running boards. At that time I preferred running boards quite separate from wings as in the earlier Vanden Plas bodies on 3 and 4½ litre Bentleys. For a lower and more modern car I liked the body of the 4½ litre low chassis Invicta, and that was the line used on the original S.S.

Not surprisingly William Lyons was right, separate running boards were on the way out and the long swept wings integral with running boards were all the fashion. A small minority of enthusiasts brought up on traditional sports and racing cars, and I was one, considered that the S.S. was overdone, apeing its betters, as one used to say. However, the beautiful lines of the S.S. had a special appeal and many of the stars

Team of Alpine S.S. I tourers, including Charles Needham in number 46 and Douglas Clease in 47.

The prototype S.S. 90, and an S.S. I tourer in the background, at Brooklands.

The same, tail view, with the test hill in the background. I took this photograph after a drive with the Hon. Brian Lewis who competed at Shelsley Walsh in it. Madly pretty in pale green to match the ERAs but absolutely no room for luggage, not even for Brian's spare pair of gloves!

of stage and screen joined the clientele. Though it was the appearance that appealed, the S.S. proved to be a sound engineering proposition as well, and soon achieved a good reputation for reliability. Though never as fast as it looked it was still a reasonable performer, and it lacked the tricky temperament of many of its faster rivals. Up to that time none of the S.S. were really competition models except in respect of coachwork competitions in Concours D'Elegance where they were great favourites.

By 1934 more private owners were competing in rallies, particularly with S.S. I tourers. I saw this at close quarters as two friends of mine, A.G. Douglas-Clease, who was the technical editor of *The Autocar*, and Charles Needham, were part of a team which was very successful in the Alpine Trial. Driving this Alpine version of the S.S., I came to realise that William Lyons project was potentially a great sports car. It was soon followed by the S.S. 90 which I drove in prototype form with the Hon. Brian Lewis who raced it at Shelsley Walsh. The Alpine S.S. I and the S.S. 90 were the cars that put S.S. on the sports car map.

The autumn of 1935 saw an important milestone in the story of William Lyon's company. A new and much improved model was produced and the name Jaguar was used for the first time. Just as surely as the S.S. cars moved up market from the Swallow bodies, the S.S. Jaguar car climbed up into a better class than the previous S.S. models.

The car with an overhead valve engine still built by Standards was the sensation of its time: a six cylinder 2½ litre developing more than 100 brake horsepower and achieving an easy 90 mph. Its appearance was very like the Park Ward bodied Bentley, but at only £395 against the Bentley's more than £1,500, no wonder it was a success. Soon there was a larger engined model of 3½ litre; and the short chassis model 90 became the 100 when it was fitted with the overhead valve Jaguar engine.

The S.S. Company was getting a hold in the sports and racing car world, but was not accepted as 'Thoroughbred'. The S.S. 100, so highly regarded today was never considered in the class of contemporary Aston-Martins, Frazer Nashes and Rileys, let alone Bugattis and Alfa Romeos. This must be almost unbelievable to young enthusiasts today; because the S.S. 100 is one of the most valuable and sought of pre-war sports cars. I do wonder if perhaps the model is coveted more for Concours D'Elegance than for driving today.

Before the war 'the right crowd' at Brooklands still regarded the S.S. as too flashy despite the fact that the S.S. Jaguar 100 soon became one of the most popular and successful sports of the late 1930s. It did not compete in the principle road races and in fact William Lyons actively dissuaded owners from entering in the more important races, because he knew that the S.S. was not ready for that sort of competition. But private owners had a lot of

A.G. Douglas-Clease driving the works production S.S. 90 in the paddock at Brooklands.

fun and plenty of success in every sort of amateur competition.

The increasingly popular saloons and drop head coupés climbed up market all the time. The smaller editions were S.S. Jaguar 1½ litre models, again with overhead valve engines built by Standards.

I was driving the various S.S. models on test and demonstration on the road and on Brooklands track, this showed me their good points and some deficiences. All had good 'bottom end' performance, both in respect of acceleration and brakes as well as handling. It was only at the top end of the performance that their lack of steam tailed off quickly and roadholding became tricky. The side valve engine always had the typical soft feel and rather hissing exhaust note.

All the S.S. Jaguar range with the overhead valve engines were very much better than the side valve cars, particularly

the S.S.100 but with that model new problems arose. With a maximum speed of about 90 mph handling was decidedly difficult and the lack of a racing pedigree showed.

Norman Wisdom trying an S.S. 100, which he purchased and re-registered NW 100

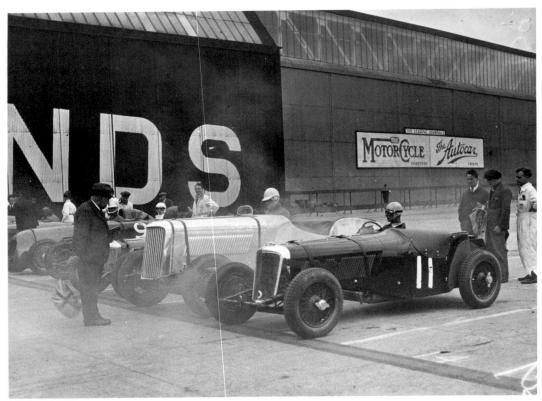

T.H. Wisdon racing the fast and much modified works S.S. 100 at Brooklands. The starter is A.V. Ebblewhite, alongside Tom Wisdon is Charles Follett in his Lammas-Graham and closer to the Vickers shed is John Appleton in the Appleton special. That S.S. 100 was, and still is, much the fastest car of it's type.

Chapter Two

JAGUAR IS BORN
– The Racing Years –

After the war the new cars dropped the initials S.S., Jaguar was a far better name and quite well established, whilst the initials S.S. had unfortunately become associated with Nazi storm troopers. Jaguar Cars Limited continued with production of the 3½, 2½ and 1½ litre cars for a time. The first of William Lyon's cars that I owned myself was one of those 1½ litre saloons, starting a long line in which I considered each successive Jaguar to be the best car of its class – culminating in the subject of this book, the Jaguar XJS.

My first Jaguar: a post-war 1½ litre saloon.

In 1948 Jaguar announced their new post war car, the Mark V, W.M. Heynes who had been chief engineer of the company since 1934 and was a director of Jaguar Cars Ltd, further developed the original six cylinder Standard engines and designed a new box section chassis with independent front suspension. As with all his cars William Lyons himself was responsible for the general concept and design of the bodies. As well as the sports saloon a fine drop head coupé was also offerred. The Mark V was priced at just under £1,000 and sold well, still a lot less costly than the £2,500 of a Bentley.

Most historians are less than enthusiastic about the Mark V Jaguar, referring to it as merely an interim model, between the pre war series and the later XK engined cars.

However the public obviously liked the car because it was in production for more than three years. Nearly 11,500 were made and in my opinion it was a splendid car. It was much loved here in England and also in America where it sold well.

My own Mark V was one of the last produced, and Raymond England, the Service Manager of Jaguars, arranged for it to be made with some worthwhile modifications. I had known Raymond, much better know as 'Lofty', for many years. Even then he had a great reputation in the world of motor racing, first with Birkin and Couper, then with Whitney Straight, Dick Seaman, ERAs, Alvis, and the Chula/'Bira équipe – to name only the principle racing organisations with whom he worked. I am very fortunate in that over the years my Jaguars have had that extra attention from Lofty England. He is not only one of the greatest, he is also one of the kindest and modest of men. Lofty arranged that my Mark V was fitted with steel connecting rods, some small detailed engine modifications and a proper handbrake, instead of the standard umbrella type that I disliked. Mine did a genuine 100 mph with handling to match and I loved it. Its only real drawback was the drum brakes which were very prone to fade, a common fault in high performance cars built before the era of disc brakes.

Not mine, but the same year Mark V now restored by Jaguars. I tried this one forty years after its manufacture – still a great car and still a great looking car, with the Lyons flare.

My mark V at Silverstone being hitched up to give Stirling Moss a tow start. Note the rather nice non-standard rear wing valances. Jaguar's styling department liked these and would have used them if they had continued with the model but the Mark V was dropped and replaced by the Mark VII with very different wing treatment.

Concurrently with the Mark V, Jaguar produced the greatest highlight in the company's history to date – the XK 120. Bill Heynes headed a design team which produced a truly wonderful twin overhead cam shaft engine as beautiful to look at as it was powerful, smooth and efficient. That unit, the XK engine has been and still is today one of the greatest engines ever produced, in my opinion even greater than any of the engines produced by Bentley or Bugatti. Much of the reputation of the Jaguar company is owed to this brilliant unit, and to Bill Heynes, now retired from the Company.

The body of the XK 120 was designed by the late Malcolm Sayer who came to Jaguar from the Bristol Aeroplane company, but it was William Lyons who master-minded the concept. The open sports two seater body was beautiful beyond words and acclaimed the world over.

I was Assistant Clerk of the Course at Silverstone for the B.R.D.C. International Trophy and Jaguars loaned me an XK 120 as my track car. It was my first taste of that beautiful cat, and I made the most of the opportunity, dashing round Silverstone between races checking that all was well with the observers and flag marshalls. Prince Philip, the Duke of Edinburgh, had a ride in the car and was very impressed.

Later there were drop head coupés and fixed head coupés almost as beautiful. The chassis of the XK was a simple but robust Rubery Owen frame with torsion bar independent front suspension and traditional semi-elliptics at the rear. The design team for the whole of the car under Bill Heynes included Wally Hassan, who had been with me at Bentley Motors Limited in the 1920s and C.W.L Baily. Harry Weslake was retained to advise on cylinder head design, a subject on which he was an acknowledged expert.

The success of the XK series – 120, 140 and 150 was phenomenal. Every sort of competition success was achieved. A demonstration in May 1949 at Jabbeke when R.M.V. Sutton did a flying mile at

132.596 mph convinced the world of the great performance of the XK. 120. Wins at Silverstone, then an outright victory in the Tourist Trophy by Stirling Moss, in a very standard XK 120, cemented the situation. The XK was equally successful in rallies, particularly in the hands of William Lyon's son in law, Ian Appleyard.

The position of the XK 120 put Jaguar right on top of the sports car world, and Jaguar ownership came to be regarded as a status symbol. Thus a marque almost derided by the knowledgeable motoring hierarchy twenty years previously, was now acclaimed as the most desirable.

My official 'track car' at Silverstone, 1951.

The XK engine was also used in a much larger saloon, the Mark VII, of rather lugubrious appearance, not a very pretty car, but again a very successful model that sold particularly well in America, where the XK 120 was claiming most of the output of Jaguar's new factory at Coventry. The Mark VII was followed by a sleeker version culminating in a very good looking Mark X.

Now Jaguar was poised to enter racing officially. Lofty England with all his great racing experience was appointed competition manager. The domination of the sports car racing world by the C and D type Jaguars in the 1950s is a glorious part of British and International motor racing history. Nearly all the great names in the sport have figured prominently in Jaguar's racing history: Stirling Moss, Lesley Johnson, Briggs-Cunningham, Mike Hawthorne, Tony Rolt, Duncan Hamilton, Peter Walker, Peter Whitehead, Tom Wisdom, Ron Flockart and many others.

Five victories in the prestigious Le Mans 24 Hour Race has been Jaguar's greatest racing triumph. Like Bentleys, the name Jaguar will always be coupled with Le Mans. In 1956 William Lyons was knighted for his great contribution to British prestige.

In saloon form the Mark II 3.8 Jaguar became the leading car in saloon racing in this country. A road going version of the D type was made, but a disastrous fire at the Coventry factory curtailed its production. Only a handful were completed so they are today very cherished Classics.

All this time the Jaguar company was prospering and enlarging and there was a wonderful spirit in the works, everyone cared. Daimler and Guys were added to the fold bringing luxury limousines and lorries. Jaguar shares seemed gilt edged.

Jaguar sports cars, and other makes using Jaguar engines, scored innumerable successes in every sort of competition all over the world, so that the very name 'Jaguar' became used as an adjective indicating superlative speed.

Having established their position and learned all that could be learned from racing – for a time, the company officially withdrew from racing. In 1961 Jaguar announced a sensational new model, the E type. Its effect was almost as great as the original XK 120 in 1949. The E type was certainly a sports car, but not for racing. Though open and drop head coupé versions were available it was as a two seater fixed head coupé that the E type made its name.

Jaguar loaned me a coupé the next year for my official duties at Silverstone. Behind the XK 120 is Mike Couper's Bentley.

Using Bill Heynes' 6 cylinder XK engine, later enlarged to 4.2 litre, the E type swept the board and was acclaimed as the best looking car of its type in the world. Some private owners raced the model and it was immediately successful, particularly in America where enthusiastic owners were always to the fore in competitions. But there were no works entries for the major events like Le Mans. However, the well known dictum 'racing improves the breed' was certainly proved in the Jaguar where every facet of the cars showed how they had been developed from lessons learned on the racing track.

My Mark II saloon and Jaguar engined H.W.M. at my house in Hertfordshire.

Chapter Three

THE XJ'S ARE BORN

Although the Jaguar company had retired from racing – for a time, when companies like Jaguar cease motor racing we all tend to forget the 'for a time'. This applied to Bentley Motors Ltd. when I was in that company in 1930 and Mercedes did the same, indulging in a racing programme only for a number of years and then retiring. Whether or not Jaguar are racing they are always experimenting, developing and considering racing projects. Jim Randall, Jaguar's Director of Engineering tells me 'racing is never far from our minds'. No wonder the Jaguar is a great car, the right attitude comes down from the top engineers and it echoes through the company right down to the apprentices.

So although Jaguar was not racing for the moment, a new engine was being placed in a very exciting experimental racing car, the sort that would be ideal for Le Mans.

Since a multi cylinder engine would be required to produce the sort of horsepower needed, Jaguar decided to go one jump ahead of the opposition and use a V12 instead of a V8. Theoretically they could have gone even better with a V16, but the complications and cost would outweigh the advantage. The V12 was based on two XK units on a single shaft at 60°. It was of course a very large and wide unit, the cubic capacity was 5 litres and it had down draught inlet ports inside the head. This massive engine developed just over 500 hp at maximum revs which was well over 8000 rpm. Though the maximum horsepower was satisfactory the power was all at the top of the rev range so a touring version for a production unit would have the disadvantage of requiring a great deal of gear changing with an unsatisfactory torque curve. This also meant that the engine would be very unsatisfactory in use with an automatic gear box. All these considerations had to be met because it was Jaguar policy for the racing cars to be basically the same as the production models, that is why there are no pure racing cars such as those in single seater racing.

This one off 5 litre twin overhead cam V12 engine was fitted into an experimental mid engined sports racing car of Le Mans type, and was known as XJ 13.

Norman Dewis driving XJ13 on the banking at M.I.R.A. This was photographed by Andrew Whyte when he was PRO at Jaguars.

XJ13 during the rebuild at Abbey Panels, after its accident at M.I.R.A.

Phil Weaver, one of those most closely involved in the rebuild of the XJ13, talking to me in the experimental shop at Browns Lane. A very impressive front view of the car.

The mid-engined body construction is monocoque and designed by the late Malcolm Sayer. The platform was made on two very wide sills and there is independent suspension front and rear on a system very like the E type except that instead of torsion bars in the front there are coil springs. There are adjustable telescopic Armstrong dampers front and rear. Behind the centrally placed engine unit there is a special ZF 5 speed gear box, with ratios 2.42, 1.61, 1.23, 1.00 and 0.846:1. Final drive is 4.2:1, allowing a maximum speed of well over 200 mph.

XJ13 and XJS.

Since this car was designed with Le Mans in mind there is a fuel capacity of 40 gallons and this is arranged in three Marston rubber tanks.

The mid-engined concept was the only possible arrangement for such a car, but not only was Jaguar out of racing, there were changed Le Mans regulations which would have prevented use of that engine. Nevertheless, the XJ 13, was, and still is a fabulous car, much the fastest Jaguar ever built. What a shame it was never raced. In the hands of Norman Dewis, at that time Jaguar's chief tester, it lapped the banked circuit at MIRA at over 161 mph, still the fastest recorded time. Later the car was crashed, fortunately without personal injuries, and rebuilt for further tests and demonstrations. Lofty England demonstrated the car to the public for the first time at Silverstone at the British Grand Prix meeting in July 1973, Jim Randall took it round at a Jaguar Drivers Club Meeting in May 1983 and I drove it soon after. Apart from that and some tests by David Hobbs

and Richard Attwood this great car has been left alone most of the time, and now the design is superceded by a different generation of racing cars. It is sometimes on show at the showrooms of the Jaguar Works at Coventry and is always on demand for exhibitions of racing and sports cars. Though with a quite different background, the XJ 13 is a prestigious project like the V16 BRM.

On the production line the E Type widened the Jaguar market and still pushed it further up market, not only in Europe but also in America. In 1963 Jaguar acquired Coventry Climax, the well known manufacturers of fork lift trucks, but famous for the production of Coventry Climax Grand Prix engines. This acquisition brought Wally Hassan back to Jaguar, as he had been with Coventry Climax for several years. With him came Harry Mundy another brilliant engine designer whom I had known for many years in ERAs and BRMs. The Jaguar front seemed all set for continued success in a fine large factory in Browns Lane at Allesley on the outskirts of Coventry, but the pattern of industry was changing. This was the age of the big groups and in 1966 Jaguar merged with the British Motor Corporation. Only two years later it became part of British Leyland, and Jaguar seemed to loose some of its identity. Those buoyant Jaguar shares lost their value and the great company became a nationalised industry. Under these difficult conditions most of the management staff and engineers (in a lesser company they would be called workers) did wonders and maintained a great deal of the enthusiasm that burned so brightly in previous years.

George Mason and Peter Dodds

Jaguar apprentices still tended to be good types, enthusiastic about the product and its racing history, thus building up the nucleus of a fine work force. It soon became apparent that the individuality and pride of Jaguar needed the scope and a degree of autonomy which was very difficult to obtain in a group like British Leyland.

XJ13 demonstration at Silverstone in July 1973. This side of the car Lord Camden, at the wheel Lofty England, on the far side of the car George Mason and Peter Dodds.

I try the XJ13, the fastest sports car I have ever driven.

Chapter Four

AMALGAMATION
– The Leyland Years –

The next period of Jaguar history is very complicated because the larger mass producer manufacturers in the British Leyland Group made big losses and Jaguar was merged with other companies with which it was not compatible. Sir William Lyons, and later senior executives, such as Lofty England when he was chairman, and Bob Knight did everything possible to retain Jaguar's autonomy, but the Ryder plan (an investigation into the affairs of B.L. by a team under Sir Don Ryder appointed by Wedgewood Benn) made the Jaguar situation almost impossible by recommending further submerging of the Jaguar entity.

Despite all these difficulties the engineering division of Jaguar managed to operate well, and the extremely successful XJ saloon range was launched. Once again Sir William Lyons was responsible for the concept of the car, though he had relinquished the post of Managing Director when the cars were announced.

Only Andrew Whyte in his fine book *Jaguar, the History of a Great British Car*, has detailed the many changes and complications of company structure that Jaguar had to suffer under B.L. administration. Andrew's staunch loyalty to Jaguar's cause has done much to educate the press and the public on the difficulties and how well they have been overcome.

The XJ saloons, the beautiful two door coupé and the Daimler versions, were all originally supplied with the well proven XK engine, but like the E Type were due for a new and much more sophisticated unit. That engine is the heart of the XJS the subject of this book.

Experience with the XJ 13 convinced Jaguar engineers that a V12 of some sort or other must be the engine of the future, either for racing or for a super-car on the road. Wally Hassan and Harry Mundy headed a design team that considered new units. A mid-engined car would obviously have the greatest performance but Jim Randell in his paper *Motor Car Concepts* states 'the best mid-engined vehicle is undoubtedly one in which the rear axle is more substantially tyred than the front axle. With the limited luggage and spare wheel space available on such vehicles this solution is clearly very impractical.' That means two spare wheels on a mid-engined car, and it is difficult enough to accommodate one spare let alone two, so a future super-car for production had to be front engined. A very wide unit like the twin overhead cam shaft hemispherical head engine, used in XJ 13, would occupy an embarrassingly large amount of space in front of the driver. A mid-engined configuration does give more latitude in this situation because placing the engine in front of the driver makes it almost impossible to accommodate the necessary arches for the steerable front wheels.

The attractive two door coupé, XJC. First produced with the XK series 4.2 6 cylinder engine and later with the new V12 5.3 unit.

Wally Hassan and Harry Mundy came from Coventry Climax where they had been engaged in a new design of flat head with a single overhead cam shaft. That type of engine could be much narrower and more easily accommodated in a front engine car. Single cylinder rigs were used to test several designs using flat heads and

Jaguar's new V12 engine introduced in March 1971. 60° V12 5.3 litre flat head.

Early photograph in the wind tunnel at M.I.R.A. Note that at this stage the car is designated XK F.

On the banking at M.I.R.A.

Andrew Whyte took charge of the press launch of the XJS and took this photo.

The original press 'impressions' days were based in the Lake District, to take full advantage of the old A6 road over Shap, now bypassed by the M6. These were the hard-working engineering boys from Jaguar, who prepared these pre-production cars for the event, which had its headquarters at the Edenhall Hotel near Penrith and took place in July '75. They were:
RIGHT to LEFT: *Peter Taylor, Digby Larque, Harry Miller, Bob Hewitt, Allan Hopkins, Jim McCranor, Peter Bevan, Jim Suttle, Gordon Gaskin, Sam Ford, and John Barnett.*
(*Peter Taylor, Jaguar racer of note and engineer in charge of press cars.)

they gave very promising results which led to the production of a new experimental 5.3 litre 60 degree V12 engine, which gave over sufficient brake horsepower on production cams, and obviously considerably more could be obtained with racing cams.

The first production flat head type V12 of this sort was fitted into Harry Mundy's series 3 E type coupé and the second went into Lofty England's similar car. These were first fitted with four speed Jaguar gearboxes and later with Borg Warner automatic gearboxes. Later Harry Mundy

had an enlarged 6.4 litre engine with a longer stroke and an experimental one-off Jaguar 5 speed gear box. That car did over 160 mph.

The flat head V12 engine gave plenty of torque low down on the rev range. So the final E type, the Mark III, was the first Jaguar production car to use the V12 engine. It was another very successful model, faster and smoother than the original E Type but not quite so shapely. Having to house so much larger an engine rather spoiled its lines.

Two of the best Jaguar rally drivers of the XK days (both Alpine Cup winners) are also long-standing agents for the marque; ie. Ian Appleyard and Reg Mansbridge. Both have commissioned individually 'customised' XJSs. This nice two-tone light-blue car was done at the works for Joan Mansbridge, wife of the Lincoln distributor.

Journalists came from far and wide to see and drive the XJS in 1975. The late Milos Skorepa drove all the way from Czechoslovakia in his splendid old Ford V8. Andrew Whyte took this picture to emphasise the Jaguar's low build.

Appleyards of Leeds offered a 'special edition' XJS not only in two tones of paint, but with a Vinyl-type roof covering, and special wheels.

No 'N' – registered XJSs were sold new, but of course pre-production cars were running long before 1 August '75!
Jackie Stewart used this one for a quick run up to Turnberry for one of those celebrity golf events.

Another former World Champion to express his delight in the XJS on its announcement was Phil Hill, which he was able to compare with the very last E type to be built (background). He was at Jaguar's Browns Lane works to participate in a film about his career; he had given Jaguar's XK 120 and C type their first big USA victories in 1950 and 1952 respectively. Joining in the proceedings was the then recently retired Jaguar Chairman Lofty England, racing chief of Jaguar back in its Le Mans days, the fifties.

Soon the V12 engine was supplied in all the Jaguar and Daimler range of saloon cars, because this was the original plan for those models. There was continuous development of the unit over the years but no great changes, and the whole Jaguar and Daimler range of cars quietly moved up the world's market place, to lie alongside Rolls Royce, Bentley and Mercedes.

For a long time the world was looking for a new Jaguar to replace the E type which had a very long and successful innings. But Sir William Lyons had a great goal in mind – the ultimate 'super-car', with all the performance plus perfect silence and docility with the most dashing and elegant appearance.

The concept of the Jaguar super-car started with the requirement that it should be a two door close coupled coupé, with better seating accommodation than the average 2 + 2, that is with more room than the 2 + 2 E type, but not necessarily with as much accommodation for the rear passengers as the Jaguar XJ Coupé. The appearance of the car had to be rakish and sporting and there must be ample luggage accommodation for four people touring. As with all previous S.S. and Jaguar cars, this had to be with the William Lyons flair – but the more so because this had not only to be the greatest Jaguar ever, but like all Jaguar cars also very good value for money. Sir William Lyons also insisted that this car must be better than any other car produced in the world regardless of price, and he was confident that his engineers and work force would be able to achieve just that. To put it mildly he was asking a lot.

Extreme docility and silence was demanded for town traffic and at least 150 mph motorway speed at the other end of the scale. Road holding and supreme handling to racing car standards was also required and at the same time the greatest possible comfort.

When the car was first produced fuel economy was not quite so important as it is today, but still a reasonable economy was required. Ever since the advent of the XK unit the heart of the Jaguar car had been its engine. This has always been so in the world's great cars. The Jaguar V12 unit was unmatched in its excellency, combining very high maximum horesepower with tremendous torque right through the rev range, extreme docility and silence, and every virtue including even quite reasonable petrol consumption. So obviously the new supercar originally named XJF, used that V12 engine.

Many prototypes were built, some were quite small models and some full size. Many variations of the original shape were tried, some were wooden mock-ups and some were complete cars which were tested extensively over large mileages on the continent. Sir William was very much in at the start of the XJS, in a sense this was his final and ultimate Jaguar success but there were difficulties ahead with its production.

The final first production XJS was released to the public in 1975, the quoted maximum power was 285 brake horsepower at 5500 rpm. The earlier V12 engines used carburetors although the engine was always intended for fuel injection, but the XJS used Lucas Opus Mk II electronic system right from the start and this provided even better torque in the lower and middle rev ranges. The all-aluminium engine used a typical Jaguar bore and stroke configuration, 90 mm x 70 mm giving a cubic capacity of 5343 cc. The single overhead camshaft per bank was driven by chain and there were seven main bearings. The compression ratio was 9-1. There was maximum torque of 294 lbs per ft. at 3500 rpm.

This type of unit requires a lot of cooling so there was a thermostatically controlled fan, a large oil cooler, and a secondary engine driven viscous cooling fan, and a Marston Superpak Crossflow radiator. The very important and severe American and Canadian Federal emission requirements were met much more easily with the fuel injection system than with the original carburetors.

After Sir William's retirement the directors of British Leyland fully realised that Jaguar faced a very difficult problem. The climate of business, not only in England but all over the world required a

Andrew Whyte shows the cockpit layout to Phil Hill. Lofty England in the passenger seat.

different sort of administration under a large group; and of course the pessimistic Ryder plan, all pointed to the fact that Jaguar needed a new boss, someone every bit as brilliant and strong as Sir William in his day.

Looking to the 80s and beyond it is a new world with quite different problems. Sir William was absolutely right in every aspect of his administration – in his day, but he more than anyone else realised, that a

new administration with new ideas was required to take Jaguar ahead to the future. How to find that man was the problem. There were several splendid men to carry on Sir William's fine tradition, but something else was needed, someone to build on to that tradition, losing nothing but adding further strength and enthusiasm in a very different modern world.

USA press came to UK and drove XJSs from Coventry to Wales and back. John Dugdale (who organised the trip) took this picture at Browns Lane of Steve Thompson (Road Test magazine) and Andrew Whyte.

Chapter Five

THE FLAGSHIP IS BORN
– Birth of the XJS –

I live in a village on the edge of the Cotswolds close to Stratford-upon-Avon and only thirty miles from Coventry. Being so close to the heart of the British Motor Industry, we often see secret prototype cars on test. In the early part of 1975 there were rumours of a new Jaguar, always an exciting prospect. The famous E type had been in production for a long time and friends told me how they had seen a new shape, badgeless and obviously disguised, which must be the new Jaguar to replace the E type. On one occasion I myself had seen in the distance, a new long low sports car streaking up the famous Edge Hill. Though it was far away I felt sure that it must be the 'new Cat'.

A few weeks later I was having lunch with friends at a restaurant in Stratford-upon-Avon. Happening to glance out of the window, I saw coming up to traffic lights outside the restaurant the most beautiful and exciting sports car – obviously Jaguar. I dashed out into the road, right up to the car. As I gazed in rapt admiration the driver lowered his window and called out 'Rivers!' Then I saw that the driver was John Dugdale, an old motor racing friend

Brian Corser (left) Jaguar collector extraordinary and driver/author Rivers Fletcher, with some of the former's Jaguar sports models. In the foreground the magnificent XKSS and (L to R) 1960 XK 150S dhc, 1955 XK140 roadster, 1953 XK120 roadster; plus 1975 E-type V-12 (Licence HDU 555N) actually the last ever built and retained by Jaguar, Coventry.

The author at the wheel of the XK 140 with Bryan Corser, the owner in the passenger's seat.

Bryan considering the leading question, 'which is your favourite?'.

whom I had not seen since before the war. That happy meeting soon led to other things, because John Dugdale was over in England testing and evaluating the new Jaguar XJS for the American Market.

First impressions are important. My first impressions of that XJS was that it was superb, a worthy looking successor to the E type. Now after experience with several examples over a considerable mileage I confirm those impressions – superb!

Each Jaguar sports car has been, and still is, a leader in its field of its time. Each one absolutely right for its day – XK, E type and now XJS. It is wrong, quite wrong, to compare the models as if they were of the same era, though sometimes one is tempted to do so. The same situation appertains to sportsmen over the years. People with long experience have a tendency to idolise the tennis players, the golfers and the racing drivers of their youth, believing that their prowess was greater than the aces of today. In truth, that is nonsense, it is well known and established that man jumps higher, runs faster, hits harder and rides further every decade. Look at the record book. So in evaluating performances of cars and sportsmen one should only compare performances with others of the same era.

Over the years advancing technology provides us with new standards that inevitably date yesterday's cars. My 1976 E type was superb in its day as is the current XJS now. The E type was a greater departure from other sports cars, and even from other Jaguars, than the XJS is from its contemporaries today. This must be so because each year cars become more alike.

The blame for this sameness is often laid entirely on general international fashions, but in fact an equal reason is the increased technical knowledge of motor manu-facturers in respect of shapes of vehicles to obtain maximum efficiency. Today we demand that efficiency, and part of the cost is that each new model is likely to be less strikingly different from the general run.

I believe we have reached a very interesting point in respect of sheer performance. At the present state of the art, 150 mph is about the maximum usable top speed for the road. The degree of concentration may tire the driver's eyes, not the car!. More or less the same applies to acceleration – in practice on the road (not in racing of course) 0-60 mph in about seven seconds or a standing quarter mile in about fifteen seconds is just about the usable limit. A good E type can do that, and there is no point in engineering a greater sheer performance for its successor. It is in the manner of its doing so that the XJS succeeds.

C type

For a certainty this car has no rivals in its price class, and that has always been a Jaguar feature. Since the scene has changed, and the very terms describing cars altered their meaning, Jaguar do not describe the XJS as a sports car, though it out performs nearly every car using that term.

In my book the XJS is pure GT, in the original sense of the term 'Grand Touring'. I think it is a shame that the term GT is used to denote many excellent cars which cannot by any stretch of the imagination be regarded as Grand Tourers. In my youth, between the two World Wars, the 'Grand Touring' cars were the great and giant Hispano Suiza, Duesenberg, and Rolls Royce Coupés and sedancas taking the nobility and gentry from London, Paris and New York to the most expensive hotels and villas on the Cote d'Azur, their ladies exquisitely gowned in the height of fashion and accompanied by mountains of expensive luggage. Well, it still happens in an XJS but not in every car that calls itself GT.

Another of the changes of today is acceptance of the automatic gearbox. An XK whether it is a 120, 140 or 150, is best with a manual box. I have used a 150 coupe with the automatic box and found it interesting, and although it worked well it just did not seem to suit the car.

When it comes to the E type you really can take your choice, the model is equally suited to either box. My own E type was a manual but for anything other than competition work the automatic would have been just as acceptable. In respect of the XJS V12 this car has obviously been designed for the automatic box. When I used an XJS with the manual box I found that I was wasting time and effort and losing much of the charm of the driving. More than any other sports or sporting car that I have ever driven the Jaguar XJS V12 is ideally suited to the automatic box. Before the days of synchromesh much play was made of the skill required by a driver to change gear, and that was absolutely true. Today however, very little of that skill is needed with a modern synchromesh gearbox. It is with the automatic gearbox that real skill is needed, changing it exactly when the driver chooses.

After a day or two with an XJS one is quite spoiled by its ease and sensitivity and finds it very hard work coping with other cars. I consider this to be a real four-seater, not only 2 + 2, four full sized people can travel in comfort for reasonable distance and there is a commodious boot for the luggage. For long distance travel and maximum performance a driver often wants some conflicting requirements. Great comfort requires softness and generous sized seats, whilst hard cornering requires a certain firmness and seats that hold one in position. On the XJS Jaguar have somehow made the best of both worlds, without any compromise. However you drive the car, for long runs or short shopping expeditions, at racing speeds or at a leisurely gait, you are conscious that you are driving one of the world's finest cars – the 'Greatest Cat'.

My only worry is that such a very fast car can easily get into the wrong hands, because of its moderate price. The power assisted steering is excellent and has a nice degree of feel, but it can easily tempt an inexperienced driver to corner at a speed beyond his ability to cope. I do not think it is a car for the very young, it is preferably for the man or woman with good experience and mature judgement – but ideally it is for the connoisseur who can appreciate its superb qualities.

Though all previous Jaguars could be said to have led up to the XJS, there is no doubt that the XK series, the racing models and the E types are the more direct antecedents. By a happy coincidence I was given an unique opportunity of looking back on all those Jaguars, comparing them with one another and the XJS. One of my nicest friends, Bryan Corser, is a well known motor sport personality and owns what is probably the finest collection of Jaguars in the world. He is well known in motor sporting circles and has done a lot of competition driving himself. He is even better known for what he put into the sport as an official of the R.A.C. and Clerk of the Course at Prescott Hill Climb. Unlike some other fanatical one-make enthusiasts, Bryan Corser drives and even owns other makes as well. In fact his daily hack is a Rolls Royce, Silver Shadow!

Even better! Very nostalgic, shades of Le Mans D Type.

Lightweight E type.

My E type 2 + 2.

I used this early XJS for some good long runs in winter weather, really magnificent motoring in the modern manner. Much as I love my 1938 TT type Alvis speed 25, it doesn't even have a hood, so it seldom gets an outing in the winter.

At the time when I was writing for the Jaguar Journal in America Bryan suggested that I might do a road test on all his faster Jaguars, and Andrew Whyte, when he was communications co-ordinator of Jaguar laid it all on for me from Bryan's house near Worcester. In ideal conditions and on traffic free roads that made a reasonable circuit that included a bit of everything applicable to a road racing circuit – that is fast and slow corners some good straights, a roundabout and even some gradients, I tested all the following cars:-
XK 120, XK 140, XK 150, Series III E type, XK S.S., C type, D type, and Lightweight E type.

At that time Bryan did not own an ordinary production E type so to complete the assessment I included my own 1976 2 + 2. Not quite fair because the earlier 3.8 Coupé was probably the best loved E type, had better handling and a little more performance. However, my 2 + 2 was a more direct ancestor of the XJS, it was quite standard with a manual box and the only extra was a Webasto sunshine roof. In blue with chrome wire wheels I thought it was very good looking, losing only a fraction on appearance to the two seater coupé. Rather more a sports car than a grand tourer, it suited me well, though rear seat passengers had very little comfort unless they were petite. Its maximum speed and acceleration was all that anyone could want on the road – in this country.

All Bryan's cars are in immaculate condition, mechanically and in their bodywork. Over the years he has taken considerable care to obtain the best possible example of each type. Then each one has been restored to the highest standard and finished in Bryan's own livery of tyrolean green with scarlet upholstery.

It was interesting to note the continuous development, so clear to see as all cars were driven one after the other in precisely the same conditions. The 120, first of the line, setting the standard; the 140 with much better handling; the 150 with disc brakes and more room; C type first of the real racers; D type, much more speed and all that Le Mans!; XK S.S., really a road going D type so of course it must be almost the ultimate sports car; the lightweight E type, a more modern racer where you can see the antecedents of the modern Tom Walkinshaw Racing cars; series III E type, every bit of performance with the V12 engine, looking towards the ultimate supercar – the XJS.

Comparing all these cars under ideal conditions and at the same time demonstrated the continuous development. It showed so clearly how lessons learned with the racing models were incorporated in later touring cars. It is certain that Jaguar could never have achieved such world leadership in sports cars had not the Company campaigned their racing cars with such thoroughness. The XJS is so obviously the resultant vehicle of a racing pedigree.

During the first years of XJS production I used 3 different examples. Two with Borg-Warner Automatic gearboxes and one manual version with the Jaguar four-speed all synchromesh gear box. My preference was definitely for the automatic, for which the car seemed ideally suited. No doubt the manual box would have been better for racing, but that XJS was not a racing car. The necessary heaviness of the clutch seemed quite out of place in that car.

From its inception the XJS has been an outstanding car, one of the greatest, but its first years were during the period when Jaguar was being absorbed into British Leyland and the Coventry Company lacked the autonomy which it had enjoyed during its former greatness. The faults were not in the design of the car, but in company with nearly all British manufacturers, not only motor car manufacturers, there was an ever increasing number of manufacturing mistakes. Quality control was lacking and Jaguar was losing something of its previous high reputation for reliability. Like most Nationalised Industries there was over manning and something was needed to restore the Jaguar reputation before the great name was tarnished.

In this country we have often found great leaders who have appeared just at the right time. As a nation we seem able to produce the right man, or lady! and what is more we seem to accept that leadership. It happened at Jaguar in 1980. Before Sir Michael Edwards relinquished his Chairmanship of BL he appointed a new and young Chairman of Jaguars – John Egan, only 42, who had been in a senior position with Massey Fergusons. His task at Jaguar was a formidable one. He needed not only to restore that which Sir Williams Lyons had built, but to build a new organisation for a very different world of the 1980's and beyond. The fact that John Egan is a car enthusiast is not incidental – it is vital. Only terrific enthusiasm and complete dedication could have brought Jaguar to the pre-eminence it holds today.

Jaguar had the finest engineers, management and work force, there was real pride in Jaguars, even the enthusiasm was present, but it was latent. John Egan recognised that he must captain a ship with the finest crew available, then they would make the finest cars, be commercially successful and the ship would be a happy one.

The early, rather spartan cockpit.

Now all that has happened. To some of us who have seen and loved Jaguars in the old palmy days and then seen a bit of a decline, todays situation seems a miracle. There is enthusiasm everywhere. They know their cars are the best and everyone is determined to keep them on top.

In July 1981 Jaguar announced a very important development of the V12 engine – the 'May Head'. Styled HE for high efficiency, the new engine was fitted to all the XJ series. Michael May is Swiss and runs his own research insititute near Lausanne. For some years he had specialised on combustion chamber shape and new ideas in connection with increased turbulance, enabling higher compression ratios to be used. After entensive experimenting, Jaguar are now using the 'May Head' on a long time licence.

The H.E. version of the XJS shows an astonishing improvement on two surprising divergent counts. Firstly the torque comes in much earlier. The same break horsepower is recorded at 3,000 RPM that was recorded at 3,900 RPM. The absolute maximum BHP is very slightly increased from 285 to 299 at 5,500 RPM. In the other direction, there is a great improvement of petrol consumption at moderate speed and no increase consumption at high speed. A 20% improvement makes the XJS a very economical car of its size. The new lean burning mixture is fed into a combustion chamber with a compression ratio of $12\frac{1}{2}$ to 1. These worthwhile improvements to the performance of the engine have in no way diminished its smoothness and silence. In fact the latest units are the most silky ever to be produced from the 'Jaguar' factory.

At the same time as the engine improvements the H.E. XJS has a number of other modifications. The most important is the higher back axle ratio of 2.88 instead of 3.07 to 1. There were new light alloy wheels carrying wider Dunlop tyres, and some minor improvements to the styling and trim. This is the XJS H.E. In my book the greatest super car and this is how it it made – an XJS is born when the sales department orders the car from the head office at Browns Lane, Coventy. Sales place the order for the body from Jaguar Cars at Castle Bromwich, with all the relevant details –

EXPERIMENTAL DEPARTMENT
VEHICLE TEST AND DEVELOPMENT REGISTER

DATE: 15.2.78
SHEET NO.5

MODEL	EXP. NO.	REG.NO.	CAR NO.	COLOUR	ENG.	TRANS.	F/NF	A/C	RH/RH	PROJECT/UTILISATION	ENGINEER IN CHARGE
XJ27	1	EHP 377K	Ex. 27-2	Sable	V12 P.I.	Manual	N/F	No		Barrier crashed July 1975	
	4	OWK 335 M	5W 1021	B.R.G.	V12 P.I.	Auto	F	Yes		Scrapped September 1975	
	6	GKV 637 N	2JB 27D	Sil. Grey	V12 P.I.	Manual			RHD	Static deflection and pressure distribution tests (6 months approx.) Series III tyre tests	J Randle
	7	GKV 638 N	2JB 27D/ 001002	Sig. Red	V12 P.I.	Manual			LHD	Sold January 1978. Now in U.S.A.	
	8	GWK 409 N	2JB 27D/ 001041	Sig. Red	V12 P.I.	Manual		Yes	LHD	Accident write off. February 1977	
	12	—	5W 1059	White	V12 P.I.	Auto	N/F	Yes	LHD	Scrapped January 1977	
	14	PWK 524 R	5W 1112	Sil. Grey	V12 P.I.	Auto	N/F	Yes	LHD	Accident write off. 27 April 1977	
	15	KHP 40 N	5W 1099	Sig. Red	V12 P.I.	Auto	N/F	Yes	RHD	Durability endurance tests	D Fielden
	16	NDU 402 P	5W 1002	Sil. Grey	V12 P.I.	Auto	F	Yes	LHD	Federal emission/Japanese spec. 1977 emission	T Crisp
	18	LDU 862 P	5W 1015	B.R.G.	V12 P.I.	Auto	F	Yes	LHD	Ducted cooling development and engine enclosure	D Fielden
	19	—	Exp.234	White	V12 P.I.	Auto	N/F	Yes	RHD	(Special lightweight panels) pave tests	D Fielden
	23	—	5W 3806	Sil. Grey	V12 P.I.	Manual	F	Yes	LHD	4000 miles emision tests on test in U.S.A.	T Crisp
	24	PWK 526 R	5W 6035	White	V12 P.I.	Auto	F	Yes	LHD	GM 400 Test & Dev.	J Randle
	25	VVC 645 S	5W 7119	White	V12 P.I.	Auto	N/F	Yes	RHD		J Randle
	26	VVC 646 S	—	Sig. Red	V12 P.I.	Auto					R Townsend
	27	VVC 647 S	5W 7505	Sil. Grey	V12 P.I.	Auto	F	Yes	LHD		T Crisp

To get it really right, a vast number of experimental models have to be produced and tested. This early sheet details some of the first 27 built!

THE HAND-MADE CAR
– The Engine –

A computer tells head office at Browns Lane when the body of an XJS is in production, then Browns Lane order an engine from the Jaguar works at Radford. That works which used to be the Daimler factory has a long and distinguished car history of engine building is now the centre of all engine manufacture for all the Jaguar companies. The plant director, Jack Randall, who has been through it all himself from foreman to service executive, was deeply involved in the preparation of racing engines for the C and D types competing at _Le Mans_.

Since the heart of the car is the engine we will see this through its manufacture. Obviously we cannot go through all the components and assemblies from the numerous outside suppliers, but a good place to start would be with the crankshaft. The V12 crankshaft is produced by Smith-Clayton Forge of Lincoln in their Weingarten Screw Press and this picture shows the hot billet being placed in the press and the second picture shows the rear of the press with the trimming press in the foreground.

The crankshaft goes to the Jaguar engine factory at Radford, which used to be the old Daimler works. The shaft has mass balanced centres in each end, which is a new technique of balancing the mass of material through 360°. The shaft is shown being ground at the centre journal as a first operation which will be used as a machining support throughout each machining process.

George Dyson is operating the Kearney and Trecker transfer machine which drills holes for oilways in the shaft.

Looking down on cylinder blocks during the machining processing.

Cylinder block about to be loaded into piston bore transfer machine

Blocks on the track on their way to assembly.

Arthur Wildman fitting centre bearing cap to block on first operation sequence on track

Tom Ryan – inspector checking depth of combustion chambers on V12 cylinder head.

Huller 42 station transfer machine – machines V12 cylinder heads automatically transferring components from station one progressively to station 42 machining various operations during process. Note the amusing poster!

Jim Goods inserting valve seats in V12 cylinder head.

Steve Hindle and apprentice fitting pistons in bore of 'A' bank of engine

Graham Harrison fitting cylinder head gasket to 'B' bank of engine.

Graham Harrison and Gary Bond fitting cylinder head to 'A' bank of engine.

Brian Thompson fitting camshaft covers.

Brian Thompson preparing to fit pulley pedestal.

Eddie Larter fitting inlet manfold to 'B' bank of engine

Kevin Jones fitting balance pipe to 'A' bank of engine

Complete engine off track ready to go for final inspection check before test

Chapter Seven

THE HAND-MADE CAR
– The Body –

Early stages of front and rear under frames which are joined together to make a complete floor.

The body side assembly is located to the main floor.

At this stage the roof is fitted and clamped.

The body shell being transported through a main assembly rig for welding.

The shell on its way by conveyancer to the body finishing track.

Soldering of body joints.

Metal finishing in every small detail.

Final inspection.

A new body shell, prior to modication into cabriolet top. Note butresses to be removed.

Ready for painting.

After pre-treatment and electro-priming the car is passed through colour coating.

Further inspection after underseal and waxing.

Body transportation is controlled by computer, loading seven cars to each transporter automatically.

At the same Radford works, the front and rear suspension assemblies are manufactured. As with the engine, many very skilled craftsmen are responsible for these vital parts. Here C. Morris works on the front suspension assembly.

B Patel assembling vertical link for independent front suspension

Terry Brooks assembling front spring assembly

Bob Hearne and Bob Warnke – front spring assembly

Cyril Morris checking end float on an independent front suspension hub unit.

D Harris setting caster camber and toe-in.

Gordon Freeman spot welding of a rear axle cross beam

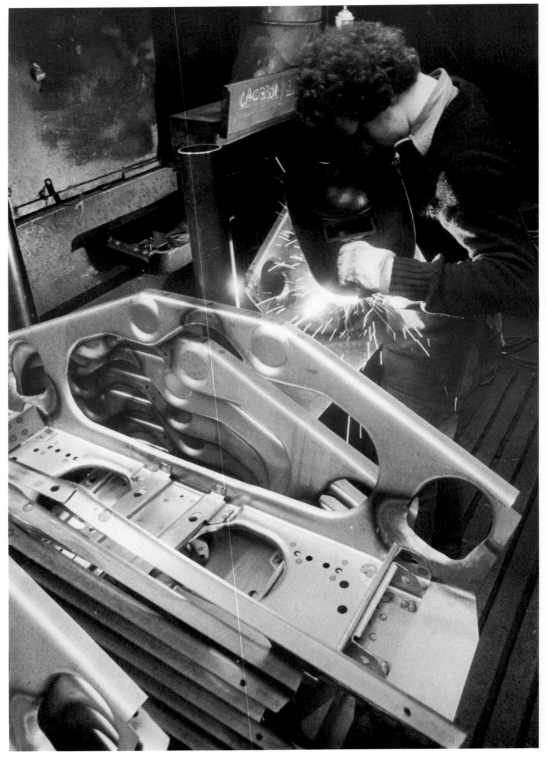

R Halford – CO_2 welding of rear axle cross beam.

W Gainford and W Tomalin – rear diff and brake assembly

W Saunders – hub and half shaft assembly

D Jones – hub and half shaft assembly

J Thurman assembling main rear suspension unit

Nigel Box – rear axle main assembly

Stillages of front suspension units complete

Chapter Eight

THE HAND-MADE CAR
– The Big Cat comes together –

At the main Jaguar works at Browns Lane the body, engine, suspension assemblies and ancillaries come together. An XJS 'sales card' is instigated with all the relevant details listed. This is the car's 'bible'. It is fastened on the rear panel and it stays with the car throughout its production life and eventually goes into the head office library.

At the main assembly build shop bodies arrive at the pre-mount track on overhead feed from the body stores.

On the static section of the pre-mount track. The high level allows the fitting of petrol and brake piping. J. Hicks, V. Moseley and K. Brewster, with 31, 10 and 6 years Jaguar experience are seen under the car.

Pipes all ready.

The body, now on the low level, has special protection for the paintwork.

J. Manning, with 13 years experience at Jaguars, fits the gearbox inspection plate.

At this stage the petrol tank is fitted.

Bulkhead harness ready for fitting.

F. Francis fitting the sun visor and headlining.

P. Allen, 14 years at Jaguars, standing where the engine will lie, fitting the brake booster and hydraulic pipes.

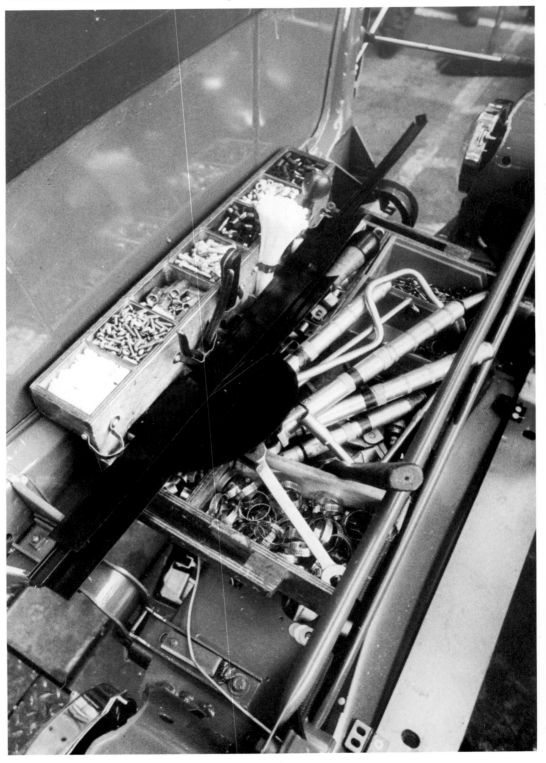

Tools required for fitting of hydraulic pipes. Note the torque spanners.

Now the bodies go up again to the mounting track. Front and rear axles are fitted.

Axles all ready in position.

K. Tallis and T. Homas about to mount the axles.

T. Bruce fitting the wheels.

With wheels on, the XJS begins to look the powerful cat that it will soon be.

The big coming together, V12 engine poised in mid air!

Singh and Lissaman lever the engine into position, tail first – the only way it will go in.

Now the steering column is in position.

Note the protective cover on the steering wheel as the gear selector is fitted.

M. Hines bleeds the braking system.

Whilst all this has been going on in the main assembly shop, John Peete has been managing the trim shop, a very important aspect of Jaguar production. Dave Turner is covering an XJS seat.

Edna Clarke sewing flute panels.

Russ Williams preparing seat frames.

David Gibbons spreading the fine leather before cutting.

Derek vacuum forming the covers.

Back on the main track R. Farmer, with 19 years experience at Jaguars, fitting the boot trim.

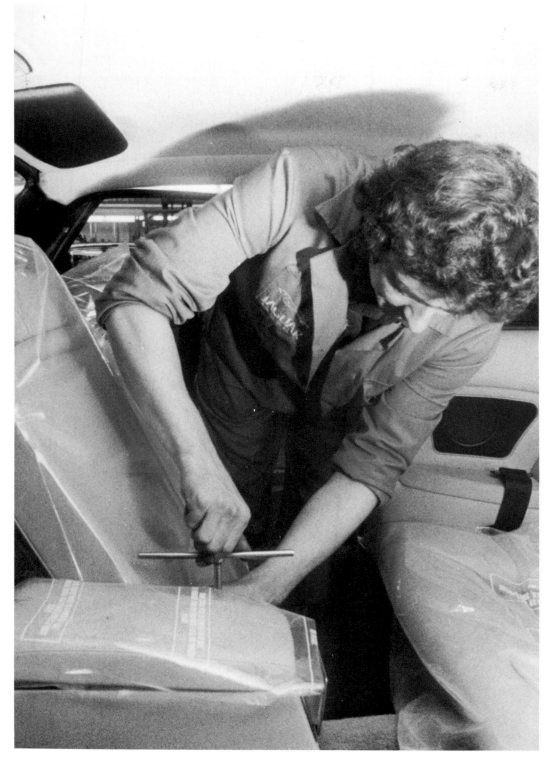

This part of the main track is called the trim track. P. Pearson is seat fitting.

At this stage there is a rectification check. F. Dove, the checker, has been with Jaguars for 15 years.

Up on the hoist again for a road wheel alignment check.

Sophisticated equipment.

The water test.

W. McDonald, 32 years with Jaguars, 'gassing' the air conditioning equipment.

Very necessary for international requirements – the emition booth.

On the final line, a spray booth for minor coachwork blemishes.

Now the body-line.

Valleting.

More checks on road wheel torque figures.

QUALITY-FINAL ASSESSMENT 2

Pass out before road test.

VARIANTS ON A THEME
– The Lynx Company –

Over the years very few companies have been successful in producing special bodies for Jaguars. The Jaguar company's own coach-building designs have nearly always been so much better than the specialist coach-builders efforts. However, in respect of the XJS one company – Lynx Engineering of St. Leonards-on-Sea in Sussex produce two very interesting and successful special editions. Lynx have special engineering expertise and are famous for their production of real replicas of racing Jaguars. Their Lynx 'D type' represents the top of the market in the specialised art of building real replicas. The cars have received world wide acclaim and acceptance. To date twenty-five of these totally authentic copies have been produced. What a pity that the term 'replica' has been so misused in recent

years describing pathetic imitations perporting to be the real thing.

Despite the almost universal use of closed cars in the fastest sports cars there are still a number of hardy soles who demand an open top. It is only the small individual companies who can produce special models in very small numbers so it would not be viable for the Jaguar company to make a soft top version of the XJS but Lynx Engineering do this with great success.

Their Spider XJS is a conversion from the standard production. A great deal of skilled engineering work is required to make this conversion because the body has to be strengthened in order to retain the stiffness of the construction. New panels and beams are constructed to reinforce the body structure, the fuel tank is modified and of

XJS H.E. Lynx Eventer.

The Lynx Spider under construction at St. Leonards-on-Sea.

An early model in the open position.

The XJS Spider H.E. with hood up.

course the whole of the hard top is removed and replaced with a new hood and frame. Needless to say the hood is operated electrically and all the other sophisticated extras are included except the heated rear screen.

On the road this topless 'cat' is really delightful in summer conditions. Not quite so fast as the standard closed production car it provides open air motoring very much in the old Jaguar tradition. Up or down the hood does not restrict the accommodation inside the car, and the appearance is very attractive indeed. Inevitably, there is a little more wind noise at very high speed in the closed position, but surprisingly little buffeting in the open position with the windows up. There will always be a demand for this type of Jaguar and it is good that a company with a fine engineering reputation like Lynx Engineering can provide this car in the relatively small numbers required.

Of course it is expensive, but such an individual car had to be.

The other model produced by Lynx Engineering is their XJS Eventer. The shooting brake body, nowadays usually called an estate model, has always been basically a load carrier and only in recent years such cars have had a sporting appeal. The fashion was really started by the Reliant Scimitar. With its powerful V6 Ford engine the Scimitar was a new sort of sports car. There were several other small scale productions of similar models including a few Aston Martins.

Now Lynx have produced their Eventer on the Jaguar XJS and it is surely the fastest estate in the world. Like the Spider it is a conversion from the standard production, so necessarily quite expensive to produce. The loadspace is quite big with 46 cu.ft. when the rear seat is folded down, but with the rear seats in normal position, the accommodation is just the same as the normal production car.

Once again beauty is in the eye of the beholder and some people consider the Eventer even more beautiful to look at than the normal XJS. It is certainly a very dashing car, and for some a more practical machine. The standard of workmanship is really excellent and I have used the Eventer in every sort of weather condition and found it without any faults from the point of view of leaks and draughts etc.

Parked in the competitors paddock at the vintage sports car club race meeting at Oulton Park, the Eventer was the centre of admiration all day. With an attachment towing a racing car on a trailer, this would provide ideal transportation for an owner wishing to continue his speedy transport on and off the racing track.

The world of sports cars and motor racing has always thrown up small companies of rabid enthusiasts that have combined work with pleasure, and in fact such businesses are really a 'way of life'. Lynx Engineering is a good example, with Guy Black who founded the company after he had been Chief Production Engineer of Westlake Engineering, and Chris Keith-Lucas. Lynx Engineering and their Derek Green personify the enthusiastic set up that produces cars only for the true enthusiast.

In the paddock at Oulton Park.

In my stable at home

Chapter Ten

THE RACING
– Tom Walkinshaw Racing –

The XJS owes so much to its racing pedigree. Jaguar engineering is born of Le Mans and the Company policy has always been to use racing to develop the production car, not merely using the name for prestige.

In 1977 before the XJS was homologated in the E.T.C. (European Touring Challenge formula) Broadspeeds ran two Jaguar XJ 5.3 'C' models. Ralph Broad and his team made a bold attempt with a very big and heavy model by no means ideally suited for racing. Top drivers were employed and John Fitzpatrick, Tim Scheneken, Derek Bell and Andy Rouse put up stirring performances, but the project was not really successful.

In the USA Jaguar enthusiasts have always been to the fore in racing. In recent years, that is since Jaguars retired from Le Mans and similar events, it seems that we have been rather shy in comparison with the American enthusiasts. Bob Tullus and his group 44 team have collaborated with Jaguar Cars Inc. in developing and racing very advanced cars for events in the States and in Canada.

Their use of the Jaguar V12 engine has been very successful, and I hope will eventually lead to the company's

Victory on home ground. Martin Brundell/Enzo Calderari/John Fitzpatrick win the Donington 500 on 1st May 1983.

involvement in Le Mans again. But that sort of car today is not much akin to the road-going vehicle. Group A in the E.T.C. is the sort of racing which is closest to the standard road-going XJS.

In this category the general exterior shape of the car cannot be altered, so the cars being raced look almost exactly like the road-going production vehicles. Group A regulations in the E.T.C. require the races to last at least 3½ hours, or cover a distance of 550 km, and at least one of the championship races is like Le Mans – a race lasting 24 hours.

In 1982 the XJS was homologated and T.W.R. (Tom Walkinshaw Racing Limited) raced two XJS's. This Motul-Akai team with a limited amount of Jaguar assistance achieved a considerable success. Tom Walkinshaw and Chuck Nicholson headed the team which scored 4 victories and 3 places in the E.T.C. series and this placed Jaguar fifth in the manufactuer's column.

This was the signal for the official return of racing to the Jaguar Company. Although the factory team retired in 1957, there was some factory support until 1963 when Peter Nocker, the German Jaguar agent, driving a 3.8 litre Mark II saloon became the first E.T.C. champion. That series started the present E.T.C. so it was very appropriate that Jaguar should return to racing in the same events. For 1983 Jaguar announced their full support for the Tom Walkinshaw Racing team on two XJS in the E.T.C.

Some have asked why Jaguar did not enter the cars themselves as factory entries. The fact of the matter is that in todays top international motor racing, the size of the operation requires a very large specialised racing department and it takes some years to train and develop such an organisation. T.W.R. already had a first class set up at Kidlington near Oxford, not too far away from Coventry. Their personnel have a fine raport with Jaguar and the good experience with their own XJS in 1982 provided an ideal starting off point for the return of Jaguar racing. For 1983 T.W.R. has a new set up at their establishment at Kidlington

Martin Brundell with No. 1 BMW right on his tail at Donington.

Oxford, with new additional buildings where the racing Jaguars are prepared. Two cars are used and there is a third machine for spares. One car is brand new to the latest specification and the second is last years number one car updated to the new specification. The third car from last years team is being kept as a reserve and for spares.

Since E.T.C. regulations limit the modifications allowed, the general specification is very similar to the standard production, but there are certain alterations which have put up the brake horsepower from 299 to over 375. There are higher compression pistons and altered cam profiles. Unlike the XJC campaigned by Broadspeed, the T.W.R. XJS's retain wet sump lubrication. There are modifications to the brakes with 13" 'Sphericone' discs all round with 4 pot calipers. As on the standard production model there is electronic fuel injection from Lucas.

The principle alteration from standard is the use of a Getrag 5 speed manual gearbox, because of course the racing requirement is entirely different from that of the touring concept. Three different final drive ratios are allowed and they are 3.07:1, 3.31:1 and 3.54:1 and these are varied to suit the events.

The all independent suspension is basically standard but of course is rather stiffer with modified Bilstein telescopic shock absorbers. The wheels are B.B.S. centre-lock alloy 3 piece of 16" diameter and Dunlop provide the racing tyres.

The XJSs are very attractively and distinctively finished in the T.W.R. livery of white and green, and from a distance look remarkably standard, but when you look inside it is very different, with practically no trim and a substantial roll cage occupying a lot of the room. They use Recaro seats and Willans racing harness. For the pit stops there is a splendid A.P. air jacking system and a large 120 litre fuel bag. The standard XJS weighs 1750 kgms. and the T.W.R. racing version is down to 1400 kgms.

With headlights on blazing his way through the pack.

The racing car development has been a joint effort between T.W.R.'s engine specialist Alan Scott and Jim Randall, Jaguar's Director of Engineering.

Long distance racing needs a very strong support team from the pits and there is a fine team of mechanics under their chief man Kevin Lee, and the team manager is Paul Davies who has been with T.W.R. for more than 4 years.

The racing team is led by Tom Walkinshaw himself who is one of the leading international drivers in this type of racing. Some of his best known victories have been in the Tourist Trophy where he has been in the winning team on 3 occasions, driving the Jaguar XJS 1982. The T.T. has always been a good event for Jaguar – Stirling Moss won 7 times. Tom Walkinshaw was first successful in single seater racing in formula Ford and then formula 3, but he is much more than just a driver, he is a brilliant technician who leads and manages T.W.R.

Walkinshaw's usual partner in 1982, and again with the team in 1983, is Chuck Nicholson from Lincolnshire. Chuck has raced in many formulae including historic racing. He was Walkinshaw's partner in the T.T. last year and before that, again with Walkinshaw, he was the winner with BMW.

Another of 1982's T.W.R. team is Pierre Dieudonne. Pierre was another very successful formula 3 driver but he was equally successful with Ferrari in the long distance races at Le Mans and Spa.

T.W.R.'s most experienced driver is John Fitzpatrick who has been racing all sorts of cars for more than twenty years. Way back in 1966 he was the British saloon car race champion and is probably best known for his successes with Porsche and Ford. All over the world, including the U.S.A. 'Fitz' is one of the most popular drivers on the racing scene today.

The Swiss driver Enzo Calderari was first successful with Porsche and then with BMW and driving a BMW he was a great rival to the Jaguars last year. He is a great friend of Tom Walkinshaws and should add great strength to the 1983 T.W.R. team.

By far the youngest driver in the team is 23 year old Martin Brundle who was, and still is, a formula 3 'ace'. He had valuable experience partnering Stirling Moss in some saloon car racing in 1981 and last year he won the top Grovewood Award for his formula 3 performances. He has already proved his worth in the T.W.R. team with his magnificient performance at Donington in 1983.

The second race in the E.T.C. series in 1983 was at Vallelunga in Italy, a very tight circuit so by no means favourable to the biggest and fastest cars. So for once in a while a Jaguar was not on pole position. However, Walkinshaw led the race until he had a mild shunt following upon a wheel failure. The second Jaguar was put out after

The TWR XJS at speed.

involvement with another car, but nevertheless Walkinshaw in the first Jaguar finished third behind the rival BMWs.

The third race was one of the most important from Jaguar's point of view as it took place at Donington in England. In practise in fine weather the two Jaguars were fastest of all and the only problem seemed to be the supply of the most suitable Dunlop tyres. On race day the weather was appalling, typical of the weather we were having in England that spring. With 5 very fast BMWs to fight off the challenge from the two big Jaguars the situation was not very promising as again the circuit is a tight one showing advantage to the smaller machines. In pouring rain Tom Walkinshaw led at very high speed and looked as though he would run away with the race. Everything went well until the first pit stop where somehow or other insufficient fuel reached the car and when the second driver, Chuck Nicholson, was at the wheel the car ran out of fuel and had to be pushed to the pits.

So the fastest Jaguar had no chance of getting back to the winning position. John Fitzpatrick did wonders with the second Jaguar which was running on harder tyres not suited to the wet conditions, then when Calderari took over with softer tyres (the last set available), he soon reached second position.

There was plenty of drama in the terrible conditions, cars spinning off in every direction and a few shunts but nobody hurt. At one period of the race a damaged car was partially blocking the course and the race was slowed by a 'pace car' whilst the course was cleared.

Quester in the fastest of the rival BMW's led but when Jaguar's third driver, young Martin Brundle, took over for the last spell a great 'dice' ensued. To the cheers of the crowd Brundel swept past the BMW and won the Donington race for Jaguar and England.

Further events abroad in the series at Pergusa and Mugello in Italy then at Brno in Checkoslovakia brought Jaguar and BMW level pegging in the E.T.C. series.

As I am writing this half way through the racing season, with Jaguar and BMW level pegging I am wondering about T.W.R. and Jaguar and their concentration upon winning. Motor racing is not an exact science, it is a hazardous and dangerous sport. The best cars and drivers do not always win. To me, and I guess to the engineers at Jaguar, whether they win or lose Jaguar are proving their worth by competing and demonstrating their speed and reliability.

The Tom Walkinshaw Racing Jaguar XJS with its transporter.

Chapter Eleven

NEW MODELS
– The XJS developed –

Over the years the world situation with regard to oil and petrol has seemed to endanger the Jaguar Company. Either shortage of supply or excessive cost has loomed large. It seemed that no sooner had Jaguar produced a very powerful, and of necessity fairly thirsty, car then there was a fuel crisis. First it was the post-war rationing, then Suez, and now to-day's International political situation and the astronomic price of petrol.

In truth none of these things have affected Jaguar sales as much as was feared, but there has always been a thought towards more economical cars. Though even when there has been the stringest situation on petrol, the largest and most powerful Jaguars have been the best sellers.

Nevertheless the oil crises of the 1970s posed a threat to the future of the V12, for a high performance 5.3 litre cannot be expected to be the most economical of power units. Expectations have been confounded, however, by equipping the engine with the Fireball high compression cylinder heads. This modification brought about a 20 per cent improvement in the fuel consumption of the V12 in its current H.E. – High Efficiency – form, and have thereby made the engine viable and in great demand so that its future is now assured.

Engine design is a constantly developing art, however. New knowledge of the combustion process, the fascinating possibilities offered by the application of electronics, new components and new production methods all combine to make it possible today to design and build even better engines. Jaguar had to consider another new engine with all the potential for future development to ensure that it is capable of powering new Jaguar models for many years to come, and have a potential for increasing enconomy.

By this time, a new engineering team had taken over Jaguar, for Harry Mundy had followed Walter Hassan into well earned retirement and the responsibility for developing the new engine had fallen on the Engineering Director Jim Randle, and his Chief Engineer (Power Units) Trevor Crisp.

The formidable task the new Jaguar engineering team set themselves was the designing and building of a new light, fuel efficient, high performance engine capable of filling two roles; as a performance engine developing more power than the XK 6 and as an economy engine applying all the lessons learned from the High Efficiency V12 to give quite exceptional fuel consumption figures.

They have achieved their objectives with a new light alloy six cylinder engine, the AJ6. In its 3.6 litre form which is now an alternative power unit for the XJS, the AJ6 has twin overhead camshafts operating four valves per cylinder in a head based on current Grand Prix practice and develops 225 bhp at 5,300 rpm. The current six cylinder XK engine develops 162 bhp in its 3.4 litre version and 205 bhp as a 4.2 litre.

The design and development of a new engine takes a very long time. It was originally intended that the V12 engine should be accompanied by a smaller sister, a 3.5 litre V8, which, with the same 60 degree included angle between the cylinder banks, was in effect a three quarter scale version of the V12 which could be built on the same transfer lines. It was found, however, after several prototypes had been built and tested that the secondary out of balance forces could be cured only by adding a balance shaft. Although a prototype V8 with a balance shaft added was built and tested and found to be satisfactory, the addition of a balance shaft meant that the engine could no longer be built on the V12 lines and this type of engine was therefore abandoned in 1972.

At that time I was having a drive with Wally Hassan in his ordinary looking XJS saloon. When I commented on the high performance, Wally merely grinned and said he would lift the bonnet when we stopped, but don't tell anyone what you see. There was the exciting looking prototype V8.

In the meantime, the idea of building what was, in effect, half a V12 in the form of a slant six cylinder engine had been under discussion since 1970. Prototypes were built in 1971 with two valve heads and with the crankcase split at an angle to the bores. Capacity of this engine, being half a V12, was only 2.6 litres, but the power output was not thought adequate and while retaining the 90 mm bore of the V12. the stroke was increased from 70 mm to 90 mm. This meant increasing the height of the block which therefore could no longer be machined on the V12 line.

The succession of fuel crises from 1973-4 onwards had made a smaller, very economical engine a high priority to be built alongside any new high performance engine. By now, 1976, Jaguar had started work on developing the May high compression Fireball cylinder head for the V12 engine in order to improve the economy of this engine. The head was showing such promise that it was decided that the economy version of any new engine should be fitted with a May head as an alternative to the high performance four valve version of the engine.

The major decision was therefore taken to design a new light alloy six cylinder engine to be built on an entirely new cylinder block line and which would be available in both an economy version with the May head and in a high performance version with a four valve head. In order that the new engine could be fitted with a May head produced on the same line as the May head for the V12, the one major constraint in the design of the new engine was that it should have the same cylinder bore centres as the V12. This in turn has meant that the new engine has inherited the generously sized seven main bearings of the V12, and therefore has great inbuilt reserves of strength.

Development work on the new engine began in 1976, and the first prototype of the new AJ6 ran in 1979. It had early been found that the engine would have to be slanted 15 degrees from the vertical in order to provide under bonnet clearance for the somewhat wide four valve head, but a major decision taken three years ago was to alter the design of the cylinder block from the wet liner open deck construction which was used for the V12 because it had initially been intended to die cast the V12 block though in fact this had never happened. Using a closed deck cylinder block with shrink fit dry liners instead of wet liners not only saved weight but also improved the torsional rigidity of the block which would have been even more important if plans had gone ahead for developing a diesel version of the new engine.

When first designed, the AJ6 employed belt drive for its camshafts, but at a later stage reverted to the duplex chain drive of the V12 for a number of reasons. Belt drive, for instance, required large diameter pulleys on the camshafts at the front of the engine, thereby adding to the height of the engine when bonnet height was already critical. Also, with a high performance engine in which accurate timing is critical, chain drive promised more precision than a belt.

It was not only the height of the engine that posed problems. The length was also critical, and although the traditional seven bearing crankshaft of previous Jaguar engines endows the new unit with great potential for future development, engines of this type are not noted for their compactness. To reduce the overall length somewhat, the oil pump was removed from the nose of the crankshaft and housed in the sump where it is driven by chain from the crankshaft.

The decision was also taken to introduce the AJ6 with the Lucas digital eletronic system that has served the V12 so well and the Lucas constant energy ignition system that has been employed for some time past on the XK6, rather than to venture into advanced eletronic management at this stage, thereby saving on development time which is always too short for the amount of work to be completed before the target date for the public unveiling of the engine. Moreover, the engine could then enter service with two tried and trusted systems, and would therefore stand that much more chance of upholding Jaguar's reputation for reliability.

The Jaguar XJS C 3.6.

The 3.6 litre AJ6 has a bore and stroke of 91 mm x 92 mm, giving a capacity of 3,590 cc and is inclined at an angle of 15 degrees from the vertical. It looks impressively sturdy, with a massively ribbed, deep skirted aluminium block that extends well below crankshaft level. Following traditional Jaguar practice the crankshaft runs in seven main bearings, and as these bearings are the same generous dimensions as those of the V12, the bottom end indeed provides an excellent foundation for future development of the engine.

In spite of the sturdy construction of the AJ6, however, the extensive use of light alloys for the block, cylinder head and sump has kept down the weight, and in fact the 3.6 litre AJ6 wieghs 25-30 per cent less than the XK in 4.2 litre form. The decision to change from the open deck block of the V12 with its wet cylinder liners to a closed deck block with thin walled cast iron liners has not only ensured a torsionally rigid block but one that also saves on weight.

Other features of the new engine are a two stage duplex chain drive for the camshafts and many of the auxiliary functions, with direct operation of the valves through bucket tappets, Lucas digital eletronic fuel injection as used on the V12 and Lucas constant energy ignition system as has been well proved on the XK engine.

A major decision was made to instal a completely new cylinder block line, this decision gave the Jaguar engineers a free hand to design a new engine from scratch, instead of being confined to a design that could be built on existing plant.

An aluminium alloy cylinder block was decided on both for its lightness and for its thermal efficiency, a light alloy block being better at getting rid of its heat than one in cast iron. It is a very rigid block with a deep skirt extending well below the line of the crankshaft, and its torsional stiffness is of course helped by its closed deck design with dry liners. Thanks to the V12, Jaguar had already gained a great deal of valuable experience down the years in the design, manufacture and operation of engines with light alloy cylinder blocks, and this experience was put to good use in the design and development of the AJ6.

An unusual feature of the new cylinder block line is a two stage infra red oven, for instead of the dry liners being pressed into position in the block by an hydraulic press,

The new engine in situ in the Cabriolet

the entire block is heated for three minutes at a time in each stage of the two stage oven so that when it emerges the bores have expanded sufficiently for the liners to be slid into position by hand.

Immediately all six liners are in place the block enters a special cooling tower where its cooling is rigidly controlled. Later in its production life the cylinder bores are plateau honed to produce exactly the right finish. A great deal of time has been spent on achieving the desired finish and for this reason the bores are honed twice, the second time to give them a cross hatched finish that will retain the oil in the bores that lubricates the pistons and so reduces friction losses.

Before the block completes its progress along the massive line it is checked time and again on the latest inspection equipment, including one that checks for porosity and another that checks the bores and grades the block accordingly so that the correct size of pistons for it are selected.

The AJ6 began its development life with a forged steel crankshaft, but about three years ago its was decided to change to a cast iron crankshaft. These spheroidal graphite cast iron shafts have proved incredibly trouble free during all the subsequent development running. The experimental department reported – 'The only time we broke one was when we dropped it on the workshop floor.'! Casting the shaft means that when it emerges from the mould it is much nearer to the final component than is a forged shaft which requires a great deal more machining after forging. Not only has the use of a cast iron crankshaft therefore reduced the amount of machining time required, it has also proved possible to machine it very accurately indeed. The cast shaft has also proved easy to balance. During the development of the engine more weight has been added to the crankshaft to reduce the internal couples, which has had the beneficial side effect of also reducing main bearing loads. This additional weight was added by going up from four to eight counterbalance weights two years ago. Any imbalance is corrected by drilling up to four holes in each balance weight.

To ensure a long life for the crankshaft, it is given a hardened skin by heat treating it by a low temperature nitro-carburising process. As in previous six cylinder Jaguar engines – and the V12 – the crankshaft runs in seven generously sized Vandervel thin wall bearings, which are in fact the same diameter as the V12's main bearings, 76.23 mm in diameter and varying in width from 24.33 mm to 30.48 mm according to position.

The exceptionally robust forged connecting rods are 166.37 mm between centres and carry die cast aluminium alloy pistons of the thermally compensating strutted type which maintain their correct clearances in spite of widely varying operating temperatures, and employ fully floating gudgeon pins with wire circlips. The pistons have three cast iron chrome faced rings, two compression rings and a micro land oil control ring as this has been found to give greater durability, being less prone to losing their radial pressure. Pistons for engines that will power cars to be sold in Europe have a slightly domed crown giving a compression ratio of 9.6 to 1, whereas pistons for cars that will be exported to the U.S. are slightly dished.

Jaguar opted for a four valve headed for the high performance versions of the new AJ6 because of the excellent breathing of this type of head at higher rpm, for the four valve lay out in a pent roof combustion chamber enables the maximum valve area to be obtained. Again, Jaguar had already gained considerable experience with this type of head thanks to the design and development work carried out on the four valve V12 racing engine of the XJ13 and on the four valve XK sixes. Both these earlier four valve per cylinder engines were designed and built when Walter Hassan was Chief Engineer of Jaguar and Harry Mundy was Chief Engineer (Power Units). This very talented partnership had previously worked together to develop the Coventry Climax into the most successful Grand Prix engine of its era which in its final form used four valves per cylinder. These earlier Jaguar engines therefore gained from the knowledge of this type of head which had already proved its worth in the hard school of Grand Prix racing which demanded the ultimate in performance from an engine.

Not surprisingly, therefore the four valve head for the AJ6 bears a strong resemblance to the four valve heads for the V12 and XK6, with a slight alteration to the included angle of the valves as the only major modification. It is of course a cross flow head with the inlet ports on the left and the exhaust ports on the right, the port diameters and shapes having been arrived at as a result of many hours of development running with the single cylinder engine.

Like the cylinder block, the new head is a gravity die case aluminium alloy casting, and with its valves and valve gear operated by chain driven twin overhead camshafts is assembled as a complete unit before it meets the engine for which it is destined.

The two camshafts are of cast iron with chilled cams and run in two aluminium tappet blocks, each camshaft having seven bearings and operating the valves direct through inverted bucket-type tappets. Another ingenious machine on the cylinder head assembly line gives a direct read out on a screen to tell the operator the thickness of shims required to give the correct valve setting. Single valve springs are fitted – the engine began life with single valve springs, went to double valve springs after a series of breakages, but then reverted to single valve springs when the cause of the breakages was found.

The inlet valves are of EN54 steel with 35.30 diameter heads and are at an included angle of 24 degrees from vertical, and the 31.60 diameter exhaust valves made from 21–4–n steel at 22½ degrees. The sparking plus is positioned in the centre of the pent roof combustion chamber.

The two stage duplex chain drive for the camshafts is taken from a 21 tooth sprocket on the nose of the crankshaft by the primary duplux timing chain to a 28 teeth inner sprocket. An outer 20 tooth sprocket on the same shaft then drives the two 30 teeth sprockets on the noses of the camshafts by a secondary duplux timing chain. The primary chain en route to the intermediate sprocket also drives an auxiiary shaft by a sprocket to the right of the intermediate sprocket, this auxiliary shaft carrying a skew drive for the distributor, a drive to the power assistated steering shaft at the rear, and on the nose of the auxiliary shaft is a pulley for the belt drive to the air emission pump. A hydraulic chain tensioners maintains the correct tension of the primary chain.

A further simplex chain extends downwards from an outer sprocket on the nose of the crankshaft to drive a rotary oil pump located in a special chamber below the front main bearing cap and drawing oil from a deep sump at the rear of the engine. The full flow lubrication system incorporates an oil cooler, although unlike previous Jaguar engines which have run at a fairly high oil temperature, the AJ6 ran at quite moderate oil temperatures even without an oil cooler. During the development of the engine considerable work was carried out on the porting of the oil pump and on the damping of the pressure relief valve in a successful attempt at eliminating noise from the pump, or resonance from the relief valve, for the low frequency sounds from these two sources can prove irritating on an otherwise quiet engine when amplified by the oil cooler.

Particular attention has been paid throughout the engine to preventing oil leaks. The rear crankshaft oil seal is a unique PTFE construction and a new metal to metal jointing process using a sealant is used throughout the cylinder block to avoid gaskets – with the exception of the cylinder head gasket and the exhaust manifold gaskets.

A belt driven centrifugal water pump on the right side of the block feeds in at two points on the side of the block, the water then circulating through the block and up into the head, then feeding back into the radiator from the front of the head rather than from the block as this made the coring of the block simpler. Although the cylinder bores were siamesed when the change was made from a wet liner open deck block to dry liners in a closed deck, distortion has never been a problem, one of the advantages of a light alloy block being that it dissipates its heat more readily than a cast iron block.

It had originally been intended to use an electric fan, but as a fan of this type constitutes one of the main energy drains on the car's electrical system, it was finally decided to use a viscous coupled eleven bladed fan driven from the nose of the crankshaft. the viscous coupling ensuring that the fan free wheels above medium rpm, so that at fast cruising speeds it is neither taking power from the engine nor spinning so rapidly as to creat fan roar. Additional thermal control, however, is provided by a thermostat giving progressive control of the fan speed according to engine temperature.

A Lucas roller cell pump with integral relief valve and non return valve supplies fuel at 36 lbf/in to the Lucas Bosch P Type digital fuel injection system. This, the world's first digital eletronic fuel injection system was first fitted as standard to the Jaguar XJS in 1980. At the heart of the system is a tiny silicon chip less than 5 mm square which acts as a fixed programme mini computer which is fed with a continuous stream of information by sensors on engine speed, intake airflow, water temperature and other significant factors. 'It then calculates the exact fuel flow required to provide the correct fuel/air mixture to meet the situation of the moment. The injectors are mounted at an angle in the six long ramp pipes, spraying into the inlet ports.

The AJ6 also employs the Lucas constant energy ignition system which incorporates a magnetic pick up in the distribution, for the system had proved to be exceptionally reliable since it was first introduced on the 4.2 litre XK engine.

The new engine has also been designed from the start to be easy to service. Any components likely to require any mainteance have therefore as far as possible been located on top of the engine, although the engine incorporates such reserves of strength that the only maintenance it is likely to require over long periods is for the oil to be changed at the specified intervals.

Finally, this new engine with its long, ribbed rocker covers with the Jaguar name spanning the front, its impressive length and its excellent finish once again fulfils Sir William Lyons' original demands, that a Jaguar engine should not only out-perform all its rivals, it should also be exceptioanlly handsome.

The two new models completing the XJS range, one described as the XJS 3.6 and the other the XJS C 3.6; internally at Jaguars they are code designated XJ57 and XJ58. The XJS 3.6 is almost exactly the same as the XJS H.E. except that it uses the new 6 cylinder 3.6 litre engine and a 5 speed Getrag manual gearbox. The styling and luxurious fittings are the same except where small modifications have been made to accommodate the different engine,

The New model with the 'Targa' top removed.

controls and manual gearbox.

There is a small but significant weight saving and a reduction of first costs. A greater and more important saving will be on running costs and maintenance. In no sense is the 3.6 a 'cheap edition', there is all the refinement and Jaguar flare. The range is provided to enable customers to have 'choice'.

Though the 3.6 is initially fitted only with the 5 speed Getrag manual gearbox; automatic transmissions will be provided in due course, thus further widening the choice. Just as surely as the 12 cylinder H.E. is best with the automatic gearbox, the 6 cylinder 3.6 is equally good with the manual box or the automatic just as with the E type. It is all concerned with the power curve of the engine. A main characteristic of the V12 H.E. engine is the tremendous power developed low down in the rev range and maintained throughout. The much smaller engine, with only 6 cylinders, also gives a remarkable range of power but of course not to the extent of the

H.E. So the gearbox has to be used more, hence the 5 speed manual box shows to advantage against the 3 speed automatic.

All this applies to the H.E. in Tom Walkinshaw's racing model, when absolute maximum performance is required, and no doubt sporting owners of the 3.6 engined XJS will enjoy use of the Getrag 5 speed box. Customers requiring less than the maximum high speed performance will find the automatic version absolutely first class and wonderfully relaxing.

The XJS 3.6 has a maximum speed of about 145 mph and will accelerate from 0 to 60 mph in under 8 seconds. So despite the much smaller engine the performance is very near the H.E.; and this is not a high revving engine, its 225 bhp is achieved at approximately 5,300 rpm and the final gear ratio on 4th speed with the 5 speed box is 3.54 to 1.

This comparatively high gearing enables the car to run at a remarkably economical rate. Testers at the works have been achieving 22 to 25 miles per gallon on give and take roads, and I believe that the technical journals in their road tests will confirm figures quite remarkable for a car with such a high performance.

The second new XJS is the C 3.6. At last a cabriolet top on a Jaguar. This is a two-seater, with extra luggage accommodation behind the front seats.

Development of the body style has been in conjunction with Aston-Martin-Tickford, where they have had unrivalled experience in thus field.

Modifications to the XJS body included the removal of the roof and rear quarter panels, and the fitment of new top rear bumpers, saddle (the panel forward of the boot lid), header rail, cant rails, B posts, and a centre bar. Associated changes involved new rear quarter windows, a new rear parcel shelf, and the relocation of the fuel filler. To maintain the structural rigidity normally provided by the roof, the cant rails and centre bar incorporate tubular steel strengthening, located at the A posts

and rear bumpers, and extending to the lower sills. Strengthening beneath the car takes the form of a transmission tunnel stiffening panel and a rear cruciform (a cross-shaped member that provides both longitudinal and latitudinal stiffening).

The Cabriolet is equipped with a targa roof which fits in front of the centre bar; the driver then has the choice of fitting either a hard panel or a folding hood over the rear part of the passenger compartment before he takes to the road.

The cleverly styled black hood is double-skinned, with all the hood sticks fabric-trimmed, and incorporates a rear window. When in use, the hood sticks are fixed to the base of the cant rails, and a series of concealed bolts secure the hood to the rear deck. The hood is closed by a simple lifting and slamming action, and locks onto the centre bar. When it is lowered, the hood stows above the rear deck line, folding way beneath a tailored padded cover.

All the roof panels and the hood are trimmed with a nylon headlining; the black

colour theme applied to the hood and roof panels is continued with the black-trimmed centre bar, header rail, cant rails and B posts.

These two new models XJS 3.6 and XJS C 3.6 together with the well established XJS H.E. complete the Jaguar high speed range.

At the wheel of the XJS 3.6 it seems almost the same as the H.E. Turning on the ignition there is the same instant but silent response, but by tapping the throttle there is the just discerning difference of feel of the 6 cylinder engine. I found that when driving with a light throttle I just could not detect any difference between this car and its large engine brother the H.E. except for the manual gearbox.

With the manual gearbox the clutch is lighter and seems to need a shorter travel than when the early X12 XJS models used their own 4 speed manual box, much lighter than the racing clutch on Tom Walkinshaw's racers. The steering and brakes are exactly like the H.E.

The 3.6 pulls away smoothly on 1st or 2nd according to road conditions. A smooth and light gearbox operation, with very positive actuation.

4th speed, which is direct, can be used for almost everything. On a light throttle the car will trickle along at walking pace and pull away without snatch. At the other end of the scale well over 100 can he held until the overdrive 5th speed is engaged.

Despite the astonishing flexibility, one feels that this is a gearbox to be used, and used joyously. At 70 mph in 5th gear there is really good acceleration for passing, but if you feel like it (and who doesn't sometimes?) you can engage 4th and simply leap forward to racing car acceleration. The syncromesh is very positive; and you can just feel the cones engaging before each gear goes in.

This is a very quiet car, even at high speed. And in fact it is only the existence of the V12 engine H.E. that prevents the XJS 3.6 being the quietest smoothest car of its sort in the world. This quietness is even further enhanced in the cabriolet version in its fully opened position when driven quite slowly. Inevitably there is a certain amount of buffeting of the wind at high speed, but far less than most other drop head or cabriolet cars. As with the XJS H.E. Lynx spider, there are always rabid enthusiasts, and hardy souls, who must have open or openable cars.

This is a fine Jaguar tradition now renewed after too long a lapse.

EPILOGUE

The XJS H.E. stands in the drive the summer sun glistening on the blue coachwork. The Jaguar looks every inch the thoroughbred big cat, which it surely is. Low and squat the XJS is in my eyes the most beautiful car. Like its namesake in the animal world, the Jaguar is lithe and strong always seemingly posed to spring forward in silent speed. It is not for the masses and was not designed for instant appeal, as were most lesser cars which have to be marketed in maximum numbers as soon as announced.

It would have been much easier to obtain instant appreciation from the press and public alike by producing a rather more conservative style. Say, an updating of the E type shape, which would have soon dated. No, Malcolm Sayer and the later stylists, produced a new Jaguar shape that would grow upon its very critical clientele so that in the eighties it would be accepted as the greatest.

Some early writers did not like the buttresses aft of the rear window and today not every XJS has these. I first saw and liked this sort of configuration in the racing Ferrari GTO, so when I saw this on the Jaguar I was already sold on the idea, and today I think the buttresses are a splendid part of the style. Though the XJS shape was new, it was still obviously Jaguar and loved for it, because no marque has a greater loyalty all over the world.

Marque loyalty is epitomised in the one-make clubs, and amongst these the Jaguar Drivers Clubs are world leaders. Within the British Club there are registers dealing with the different models, and XJS comes within the XJ Register, under its chairman Trevor Lang. One of the greatest benefits of the one-make clubs is information and assistance with regard to old models no longer in production. So looking far ahead, one can be certain that future XJS owners will be sure of fine backing by the Jaguar Drivers Club through the XJ Register.

In the United States and in Canada the Jaguar Drivers Clubs have always been splendid organisations, and much helped by John Dugdale and his close contact with the company in England.

The XJS is quite a large car but compact, almost 16 feet long and ten feet six inches wide, about four feet in height and looking even lower. Distinctive from every view point, but perhaps rather less instantly recognised from the front than from side and rear views.

The large doors unlock and swing open with that perfect smoothness which betokens craftsmanship. There is that faint aroma of fine leather as one settles in the driving seat. The adjustment of the seats and the length of steering column gives an ideal driving position, with a commanding view over the wide bonnet.

When inserting the ignition key and starting the engine one has to remember to watch the rev counter. For even if you tap the throttle to increase the revs you cannot hear the engine running. It is only the rev counter that shows that the engine has started, This, on one of the most powerful, production cars in the world. That sort of silence one would imagine possible only in the most expensive Royal limousine.

All the controlls and dials are set in a very clever combination of matching burr walnut and fine leather. Earlier models I had been using were rather more spartan without traditional walnut. But it seems appropriate to have the fine wood veneer on a Jaguar underlying the quality of the machine.

The effortless Adwent power steering makes manoeuvring childsplay but neverthless there is just the right amount of feed-abck to give proper feel in the handling. There is a certain tautness that seems to come only from marques with a racing pedigree.

The latest general Motors THM 400 three speed automatic gearbox is beautifully smooth. This gearbox gives you the best of both worlds in that if you are lazy or wish to concentrate on conversation with your passenger or listening to the radio or favourite cassette, then you can leave the box to itself. It will select the appropriate gear so smoothly that you do not consider or even known that it happens.

On the other hand there is wonderful scope for the expert. With experience and judgement you can make the changes when you wish to do so.

One often hears of the enthusiastic but inexpert driver who complains that the automatic gearbox keeps on changing gear at the wrong time. On a cross country run which included every sort of road conditions, Stirling Moss demonstrated to me why he prefers automatics. He varied his throttle opening with such skill that he was always in the gear of his choice, and only on rare occasions resorted to the 'hold' on a lower ratio. Though we cannot hope to use Moss expertise, it is certainly worthwhile endeavouring to emulate his skill. In a similar way the vintagent exercises his skill changing gear in his car of the twenties with a 'plain' gearbox built before the era of synchromesh.

The Jaguar is geared for a maximum speed of over 150 mph. It would have been quite easy to have provided a rather higher maximum but quite pointless on the road. As it is the XJS is the fastest car of its sort in the world. Whether you achieve 152, 155 or even a little more depends on the conditions. In any case you are still below the red line on the rev counter. In every respect the car is well within its capabilities. Continuous driving on 'autobahn' conditions at over 140 mph may tire the driver because of the degree of concentration needed with ones eyes, but it does not tire the car. It does not get hot, noisy, or show any sign of strain. Returning to pottering through a congested town, the Jaguar is just as quiet and perfectly mannered, and gives no indication of its previous speed.

I believe that perhaps this facet of the car demonstrates its engineering excellence better than any other attribute. There are a few other cars which have terrific high performance but none can combine this with the exquisit manners of the Jaguar when pottering even after a very high speed run.

Alan Randall, the secretary of the XJ Register of the Jaguar Drivers Club, with his 1976 XJS. This car has covered more than 65,000 miles and has been up-dated with the GM 400 gearbox and later road wheels. A very enthusiastic owner.

Roadholding is outstanding, so much so that I could not discover its cornering limit on the road. Even on some open curves that I know well, and am used to when testing other sports cars, I found the XJS rock steady and obviously not on its limit, when I drove as fast as I dared. Only on Silverstone circuit and Donington Park could I reach any thing like its cornering limit. On a damp Silverstone and a dry Donington, entering the curves at speed there was a nice degree of understeer enabling me to set up a drift, then well before the apex, opening the throttle, I was able to leave the corners on power, lessening the understeer as desired and converting to oversteer by using more throttle thus tightening the corner. All smooth and viceless, the XJS, despite its size and weight, handles very like a single seater racing car.

Though power steering is usually regarded as a disadvantage in very high speed cornering, I believe that in the XJS the power steering is a real benefit. The technique certainly needs to be learned, the delicate touch is an acquired art. When learned, an acccuracy of steering is achieved that could not be acquired with the brute force that would be necessary if unassisted steering was used.

All this applies to use on the road. For racing where ultimate cornering is required, the T.W.R. Jaguars do not use power assisted steering. Their professional racing drivers cope with the extra heaviness at slow speed because they are only really concerned with the handling at the highest speeds. In any case the concentration and effort required in racing is miles beyond anything used on the road.

Ever since pioneering disc brakes in sports racing cars Jaguar have led the way in providing superb braking in their cars. The XJS is quite faultless in this respect. Even the hand brake, with a very clever but simple parking device, is quite effective were many other all-disc arrangements are unsatisfactory.

I well remember 30 years ago when Jaguar saloons were coming up towards Bentley and Rolls Royce standards, the big difference was that the Jaguar was much more tiring to drive on very long distances. Only Bentley and Rolls Royce had that lightness of feel that somehow made for relaxation and tirelessness. Now Jaguar have even surpassed that quality. I have never known such ease, silence and relaxation in long distance touring whether pottering or travelling at very high speed.

Giving talks and film shows to motor clubs and other organisations all over the country I am frequently asked 'what is your favourite car?' I have to admit that, in a sense, my favourite cars are all famous vintage racing cars. But I have no doubt whatsoever of my favourite road car today, even if price was of no account at all – I admit that I have not driven every single car that could be considered a rival, but I have tried all those that I personally would consider. My favourite is, of course, the 'boss cat', Jaguars 'supercar', the XJS.

To savour this car to the fullest, a man needs to have the companion of his choice, beautifully gowned of course, and a really fast and long drive to a wonderful venue – say from Belgravia to the Cote d'Azur, or at the right time of the year, to Le Mans where the populace would appreciate its magnificent past, present and future.

SPECIFICATION X.J.S. HE

Engine: 5.3 litre.
Type: V-12
Configuration: 60° 'Vee' 12 cylinder.
Bore: 90mm.
Stroke: 70mm.
Capacity: 5345cc.
Compression ratio: 12.5:1.
Cylinder head: Two aluminium cylinder heads. One camshaft per bank. In-line inlet and exhaust valve. High Efficiency combustion chamber design.
Cylinder block: 'Open-deck' aluminium alloy block with slip-fit cast-iron cylinder liners.
Pistons: Aluminium alloy.
Lubrication: Epicyclic crescent-type oil pump.
Fuel supply: Lucas Digital Electronic Fuel Injection system. 95 octane four star.
Transmission: GM 400 three speed automatic gearbox. 'Powr-Lok' limited slip differential.
Wheels: Cast alloy wheels size: 6.5JK rim 15" diameter
Tyres: Size 215/70 VR15.
Battery: Negative earth AC Delco Freedom 'No Maintenance' battery
CP 13/11 Pacemaker

Exhaust system: Part stainless steel.
Cooling system: Water pressurised.
Impeller pump belt driven off crankshaft damper.
Suspension: Front: Fully independent semi-trailing wishbones and coil springs, 'anti-dive' geometry.
Telescopic dampers. Anti-roll bar. Rear: Lower transverse wishbones with driveshafts acting as upper links. Radius arms. Twin coil springs. Telescopic dampers. Rear anti-roll bar.
Brakes: Servo-assisted discs all round. Ventilated front discs. Safety split front and read hydraulic circuits. Steering: Power assisted rack and pinion with energy absorbing column.
Instruments: Speedometer, tachometer, fuel gauge, water temperature gauge, oil pressure gauge, battery condition gauge.
Warning lights: Main beam, hazard warning ignition, handbrake, low brake fluid level, oil pressure, direction indicators, rear foglamps, low coolant, heated rear window, seat belts not fastened, bulb failure.

Primary Safety Features

Wide section low profile steel braced radial ply tyres on special safety profile wheel rims. Servo assisted disc brakes all round with ventilated discs at front and safety split hydraulic circuits to front and rear. Fluid loss sensor activates a warning light. due to any failure in either the front or rear circuit.
Wide track and low centre of gravity for greatest possible overall stability. 'Anti-dive' front suspension geometry for longitudinal stability, particulary under heavy braking. Power assisted rack and pinion steering, for ease and precision of control. Large window area with slim pillars for good all-round visibility. Electrically heated rear window. Large area sidelamps and direction flashers. Rear foglamps. Large area interior rear view mirror with anti-dazzle secondary position and remote control exterior door mirrors.

Secondary Safety Features

An immensely strong body centre section. Front and rear ends designed to provide progressive deformation characteristics to absorb the energy of impact. Burst-proof locks on all doors. Impact-absorbing surround to instrument panel. Energy absorption device on steering column, to cushion impact of body on steering wheel under severe impact loads. Fuel lines located in the structure in such a way as to minimise the chance of fracture. Universal joints between upper and lower steering columns and collapsible mountings allow displacement in a collision. Head restraints are provided for the driver and front passenger. Spring loaded 'break away' holder for rear view mirror. Inertia reel front seat belts fitted operated by one hand. Recessed petrol filler flap (opening inwards, concealed beneath separate flush fitting cap, reduce loss of fuel in event of accident. Hazard warning system utilising all four direction flashers. The mounting of the steering rack on the rear face of the suspension beam in a position of maximum protection.

Dimensions

Dimensions: Overall length: 186.73in (474.4cm). Rear track: 58.6in (149cm). Overall height: 49.6in (126cdm). Front track: 58.0in (147cm). Overall width: 70.6in (179cm). Wheelbase: 102.0in (259cm).

Body and interior: Wrap around chrome and rubber bumpers. Forward hinged bonnet. Special twin coachline. Medallion bonnet badge. Laminated windscreen, tinted glass. Heated rear window with timer. Electrically operated windows. Twin electrically operated door mirrors. HE badging. Alloy wheels. Halogen headlamps. Central armrest utilising lid to cubby box. Seats, console, door casings, head restraints, rear ¼'s all leather. Burr elm inserts to fascia, door top rails and switch panel. Moulded rubber heel mat. Toolbox. Door opening warning/puddle lights. Inertia reel seat belts. Philips 990 micro-computer controlled stereo radio and cassette player. Steering column mounted stalks with intermittent/flick wipe.

Electric clock.

Courtesy lights. Cigar lighter. Individual ashtrays front and rear. Electric aerial. Sisal trimmed boot. Metallic paint. Central door locking. Rear foglights.

Optional extras

Cloth trim (at no extra cost). Cruise control. Rear seat belts – static. Headlamp wash/wipe.

The XJS HE at home.